Bobbin Lace Bookmark:
A Modern Take on an Old-World Craft

Cori Large

Notes Page:

Bobbin Lace Bookmark:
A Modern Take on an Old-World Craft

Copyright Page

Printed in the United States of America.

Copyright © 2015 Cori Large

All rights reserved. This book or any portion thereof may not be reproduced or used in any manner whatsoever without the express written permission of the author or publisher except for the use of brief quotations in a book review.

1st edition Print ISBN: 978-1-7333717-0-4
2nd edition Print ISBN: 978-1-7333717-2-8
eBook ISBN: 978-1-7333717-1-1

Unless otherwise stated, all photos were taken by Ramos Studios. Photos cannot be reproduced without the express written permission of Ramos Studios or the author except for the use for a book review.

Dedication

To the late Margaret Baer (1920–2014), my friend and bobbin lace teacher.
You carried on doing your thing, even at 94. You're missed by many.

Notes Page:

Contents

What Inspired This Book?	8
Author's Note	9
History of Bobbin Lace	11
Bobbin Lace Basics	14
How to Create the Bookmark Template	16
Recommended Equipment & Setup Instructions	20
Let's Make a Bookmark!	32
Recommended Books & Other Resources	103
Bibliography	105
About the Author	107

What Inspired This Book?

In the early 2000s, a children's movie was released called *Madeline Lost in Paris*. In the movie, Madeline's "uncle" comes to get her and take her home, but it turns out he's a con man who is gathering orphans for child labor in factories.

What does this have to do with bobbin lace? Well, Madeline is forced to work in a factory that makes lace using bobbins. Ever since seeing that movie, I'd been fascinated with what type of lace making that was—but it wasn't until 2012 that I learned the details.

My grandma and I went to a craft demo at my local public library where artisans would show off their work. In one of the rooms, the Polk County Fiber Guild had set up various fiber crafts for display. I saw Ms. Margaret's bobbin lace pillow from across the room. I'm semi-ashamed to say I rushed my grandmother, who was in a wheelchair, over there just to find out what that craft was. A woman named Laurie, who was crocheting at the time, paused her crocheting and explained what bobbin lace was. She invited me to one of the guild meetings.

From there, I made more friends and began regularly attending guild meetings and the monthly bobbin lace get-together held at Ms. Margaret's house. Ms. Margaret was something else. When I started learning Bobbin Lace from her, she was in her late 80s. Her patience and guidance made learning this [dying] art more of a joy.

Sitting around Ms. Margaret's dining room table learning the initial stitches, struggling through the first corner until the rows became repetitive. Our monthly Bobbin Lace meetings were often a handful of people who wanted to sit around and chat while we crisscrossed the bobbins and threads. In the event a mistake was made, the first thing we were told was to stay calm. Getting flustered meant risking the threads becoming more tangled. Being able to read the threads and determine which was on top to reverse the stitch was the most important lesson.

Aside from the monthly meetings and working on my bobbin lace at home, I would demonstrate this Old-World Craft at the Good Ol' Days Festival in Homeland, Florida. The Polk County Fiber Guild was invited down each year to demonstrate knitting, crochet, spinning, weaving, rug hooking, and of course, bobbin lace. Rug hooking and bobbin lace were the rarer of the crafts demonstrated. It was fun to educate children and adults about this hundreds-years-old craft.

Author's Note

The pattern in this book is the first one I learned how to make. One of my favorite threads for making this is Bernat Handicrafter Crochet Thread in the seashore colorway. Once you've completed one of the bookmarks, you'll see it looks like that beautiful spot where the beach and ocean meet.

I wrote this book so that everyone, even those who don't have a fiber guild or a lace guild near them, can still learn an old-world craft. There are Notes Pages throughout the book so you can make notes as needed. There is also extra space around each set of bobbin pair instructions in order to keep all steps for those pairs together for clarity.

Notes Page:

History of Bobbin Lace

Figure 1 Taken at the Doge Palace, Venice, Italy 7/15/2018 by Cori Large

Figure 2 Taken at the Doge Palace, Venice, Italy on 7/15/2018 by Cori Large

Let's start with a basic definition of lace. "Loosely defined, lace can be any non-woven, light, openwork fabric, but in historical terms it was created by using two tools: the needle and the bobbin."[1] While most people have heard of lace in general, many have never heard of *bobbin* lace. So, what is it?

Bobbin lace is a style of lace making dating "back to the fifteenth century"[2] that uses intricately interwoven threads attached to wooden bobbins[3]. Making a piece of lace is tedious, taking as long as an

---

[1] Pamela A. Parmal, "Lace," in *Encyclopedia of Clothing and Fashion*, vol. 2 (Detroit, MI: Charles Scribner's Sons, 2005), pp. 323-327, https://link-gale-com.db22.linccweb.org/apps/doc/CX3427500351/WHIC?u=lincclin_pcc&sid=WHIC&xid=ad46205b)
[2] The Reader's Digest Association, Inc., "Bobbin Lace," in *Reader's Digest Complete Guide to Needlework* (Pleasantville, NY: The Reader's Digest Association, Inc., 1979), pp. 426-434)
[3] Ann Barry, "Shopper's World; Handmade Lace from Normandy," (*New York Times*, October 13, 1985)

hour to make an inch of lace. Bobbin lace has had additional names throughout its history, as bobbins been made from a variety of materials, including wood, bone, and ivory. (If someone couldn't afford traditional bobbins, there were ways to improvise: nails with large heads, old-fashioned clothes pins, or a dowel with a notch cut into one end.) In the earliest years, bobbin lace was referred to as *bone lace*, as it was believed bobbins were made out of small bones[4]. Another term for bobbin lace is *pillow lace*[5].

The two earliest places lace making happened were in continental Europe: Venice, Italy, and Flanders, Belgium. From there, the craft really took off. Indeed, the French lace-making industry started as a way to keep money in France. The French royal court was spending so much money on Venetian and Flemish lace that King Louis XIV brought lace makers to France. Bayeux, France (yes, the same city as the famous tapestry), is the former bobbin lace capital of the world. So, while it may have started in Italy, France later dominated the industry.

> "For generations, handmade lace was a flourishing industry in Europe, employing hundreds of thousands of workers. From the 16th to 18th centuries, lace was a coveted luxury, rivaling fine jewelry. Many royal coffers nearly went bankrupt satisfying kings' and queens' appetite for it"[6].

The number of lace makers decreased dramatically in the mid-eighteenth-century, though, when a new lace-making technique was introduced. This new technique was called Nottingham lace, and this lace wasn't made by hand with bobbins but instead woven on a machine! There is an important difference between handmade lace and machine-made lace: machine-made lace will unravel if a thread is pulled; handmade lace doesn't do that[7]. And as usually happens with fads, when the ability to create lace on a machine appeared (meaning lace could be produced faster and at a lower cost), the desire to have lace on every piece of clothing waned. The exceptions to this were undergarments and wedding gowns.

Despite the invention of Nottingham lace, handmade lace was revived in Italy, and its popularity spread once again. Over one hundred thousand people were still making lace for a living worldwide in the nineteenth century. Due to the lack of child labor laws, it wasn't uncommon for children as young as five years old to be found working in lace-making factories. Even though children were capable of making lace, the creation of such items was still difficult and tedious, which caused the fabric to stay quite expensive and thus be available only to those with wealth and status. Due to the basic law of supply and demand, which essentially states that low supply and high demand lead to an increase in price (as demonstrated in handmade lace being available only to the wealthy), new ways of making lace faster and cheaper were continually being thought up to fulfill the market needs. This race to produce more lace to sell most likely encouraged the use of children in factory labor. But again, as factories were able to produce more lace for a lower cost and machines became the norm, the need for workers trained in handmaking lace dwindled.

Surprisingly, in the 1980s, lace making experienced another resurgence in interest. This occurred in America, of all places. The resurgence has gone global now. There's even an organization call the International Organization of Lace, Inc. with chapters all around the North American continent, England, and Australia.

---

[4] Kathleen Rogers, "The Labyrinths of Lace," *Women's Art Magazine*, November 1991, pp. 16-17, http://link.galegroup.com.db22.lincnweb.org/apps/doc/A262786608/AONE?u=lincclin_pcc&sid=AONE&xid=bf193b3c)
[5] Rogers, "The Labyrinths of Lace," 16.
[6] Ellen Byron, "Delicate Task: In India, Women Work to Preserve the Craft of Lace; Even with Low-Cost Labor, Making It by Hand Is a Difficult Business; Keeping Dust, Chickens Away," *Wall Street Journal*, February 14, 2006, https://doi.org/http://db22.lincnweb.org/login?url=https://search-proquest-com.db22.lincnweb.org/docview/398952341?accountid=40333)
[7] Barry, "Shopper's World; Handmade Lace from Normandy," XX12.

Once upon a time, lace makers and pattern designers were kept apart so no one person knew the entire process. My, how times have changed! Now apprentices learn the entire process during a three-year internship. If you want to get certified to make bobbin lace, there are two different courses to look into. One certificate certifies you as a lace maker, whereas taking the additional forty-hour course load will set you up to be a professional lace seller. What is entailed in this additional forty-hour course? "Lacemaking, theory, and pattern preparation"[8].

---

[8] Barry, "Shopper's World; Handmade Lace from Normandy," XX12.

Bobbin Lace Basics

There are four main equipment requirements that do not change no matter what style of bobbin lace you're doing: bobbins, thread, the pattern, and a mounting pillow. Other helpful materials include straight pins and a cover cloth. The straight pins are pinned at the apex of the half-stitch (or the X on the graph paper). The cloth is used to protect the pins, lacework, and pillow when not in use. To keep the tension on the lace, glass beads are also added to the ends of the bobbins to act as weights. The beads are optional but can make the in-progress project look attractive and colorful.

Bobbin lace patterns, also called prickings, used to be written out on parchment paper, which was quite durable. Graph paper is used today because the grid is done for you already. The X intersections are where you place a pin to hold the stitch in place. "A fairly uncomplicated pattern may utilize as few as 52 bobbins"[9]. (The simple bookmark pattern in this book uses only 20 bobbins.) "Geometric patterns [are] made with a few pairs of bobbins, [where as] complex floral and pictorial designs [can be] requiring hundreds [of bobbins]"[10].

If you compare it to modern pieces, Venetian lace is much thicker than what is made today. This is possibly due to all threads being spun on spinning wheels by hand and not on a machine. If you've ever seen fiber being spun, either on a spinning wheel or on a drop spindle, the yarn/thread isn't consistent in thickness at times. Modern technology has removed the inconsistency of hand spun. All threads and yarns are an even thickness.

But if you choose to stick as close as possible to tradition, use silk or linen threads[11]. And be aware that "traditional Bayeux lace [was] white, ecru, and black"[12] in color. Modern bobbin lace, though, is often done with crochet cotton thread, which is available in a variety of colors.

---

[9] Barry, "Shopper's World; Handmade Lace from Normandy," XX12.
[10] The Reader's Digest Association, Inc., "Bobbin Lace," 426.
[11] The Reader's Digest Association, Inc., 426.
[12] Barry, "Shopper's World; Handmade Lace from Normandy," XX12.

By the early 2000s, lace makers were still reproducing patterns from the Renaissance Era. These pieces are so authentic looking that collectors are fooled into thinking they are rare and antique pieces[13]. Even in Bayeux, France, where the city and surrounding areas once supported up to five thousand lace makers, only a couple handfuls remain.

---

[13] Parmal, "Lace, 326.

How to Create the Bookmark Template

Being able to make the template we're going to be using means that you can make a fresh copy whenever you wear out the current one.

Materials Needed:
- Graph paper, 8½" x 11", with the 5x5 quad grid, preferably with no holes
- Pencil
- Ruler or straight edge, to be used at the end
- Black, fine-point pen

Instructions:
1. Turn the sheet of graph paper diagonally to face you.

2. Count down the rows in the top corner until you come to a row where there are 6 diamonds across the row.

3. Draw a horizontal line through the middle of 4 of those 6 diamonds using your pencil.

4. From the edge of the 2nd diamond (the first one you drew a line through), draw a line slowly down the page, through the grid, and all the way down to the end of the graph paper. I don't recommend using a ruler for this because the line doesn't line up properly with a ruler. Ironic, huh?

5. Repeat the Step 4 for the outside edge of the 4th diamond on the opposite side.

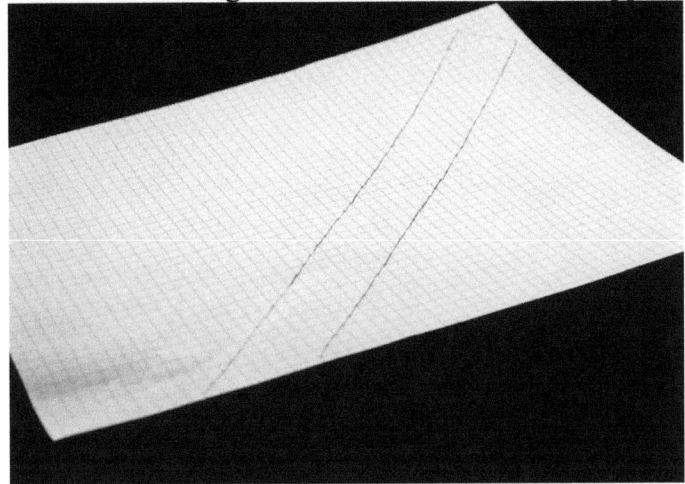

6. Count through the diamonds from top to bottom until you reach 34. Row 34 is the end of the template.

7. Draw a line across Row 34 to mark the end. Erase any pencil marks past the 64th row.

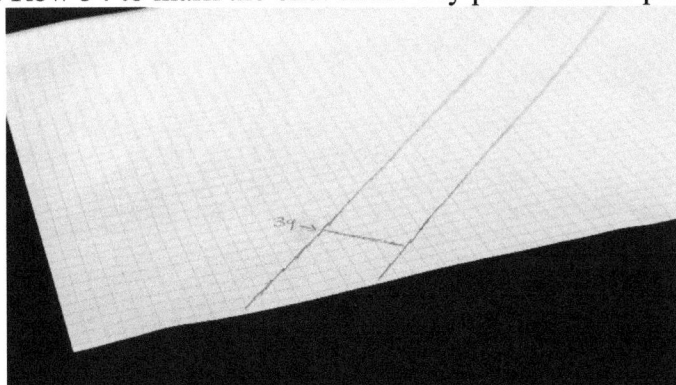

8. Using your ruler, you can go back over the lines and officially straighten them up. This step is completely optional.

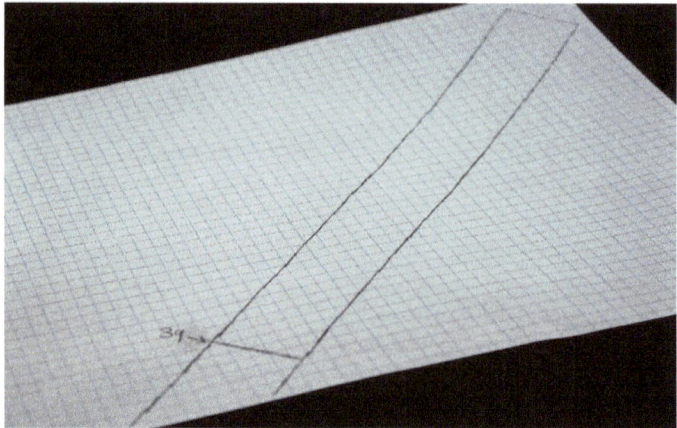

9. Using your black, fine-point pen, trace over the lines you've just drawn. This will help the edges stand out.

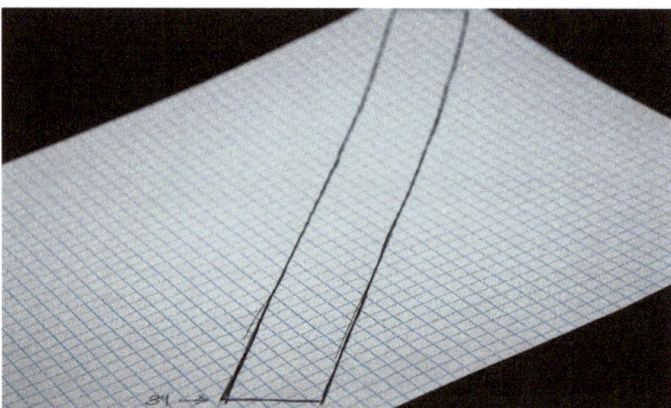

10. Using your pen, mark the dots from the image below onto your template. These are the beginning points for the pattern in the coming chapter.

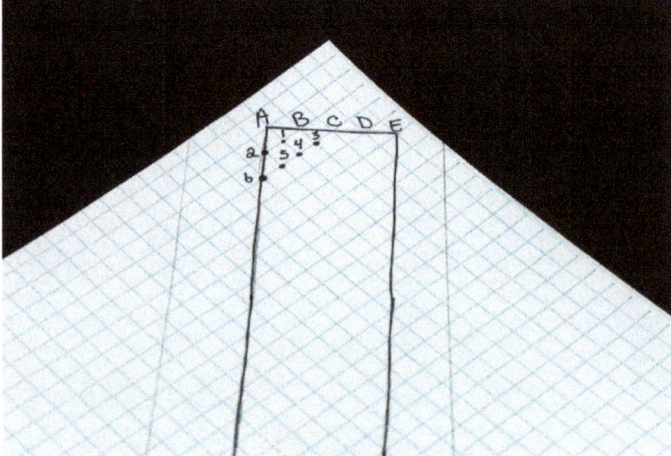

11. Trim the template down, leaving a half inch of space on either side.

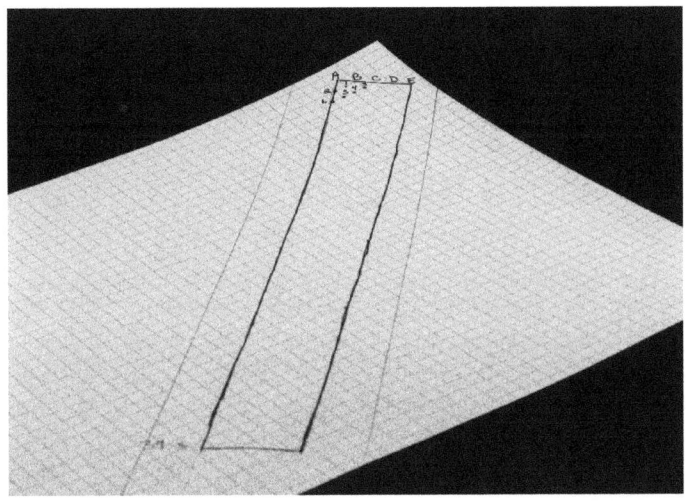

Return to these instructions as many times as you need when you decide to make a fresh copy of the template.

Recommended Equipment & Setup Instructions

There are many different styles of bobbin lace, but we're going to get started with a bookmark design that has a very simple pattern.

<u>Materials Needed:</u>
- 1 very stiff pillow or piece of foam board
- 20 bobbins—either the traditional kind or homemade ones (nails, clothespins)
- A large box of Straight pins measuring 1–2 inches in length (quilting pins with large heads are highly recommended)
- Crochet cotton thread in desired color(s)
- 1 sheet of 11" x 17" graph paper
- Pencil
- Scissors
- Fine-point permanent marker

<u>Numbering Your Bobbins:</u>

I recommend purchasing the cube bobbins over the round or oval ones. It's easier to number them. I numbered my bobbins when I first started learning bobbin lace so I could keep track of the four bobbins I was working with at the time.

When I decided to put this pattern workbook together, having the bobbins numbered already helped clarify which two sets of bobbins were needed for each step of the pattern.

1. To number the bobbins, take your fine-point permanent marker and number each bobbin 1–20.

2. I write the number on all four sides so avoid confusion when the bobbins turn themselves—yes, this does happen.

<u>Prepping the Threads:</u>

There is a very simple way of measuring the amount of thread needed to complete this project:

1. Take the end of the crochet thread, hold it under your chin with one hand, pick up the tail of the thread with your other hand, and straighten your arm out to the side.

2. Drop the end under your chin and transfer the thread in your extended hand to your other hand and repeat the process twice more. Cut the thread after the third measurement.

3. Hold the two cut ends of the thread between your index finger and thumb, and pick up the other end with your free hand.

4. Drop the cut ends. Catch the middle of the thread with your index finger and pinch the thread together with your thumb and middle finger.

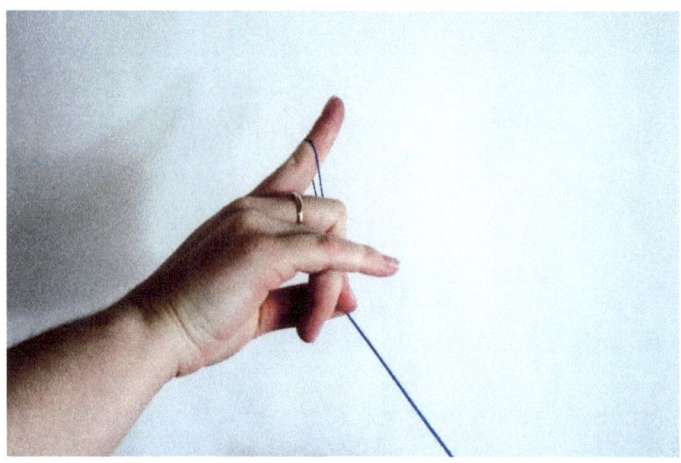

5. Tie a knot where the threads are pinched to create a loop about two inches long.

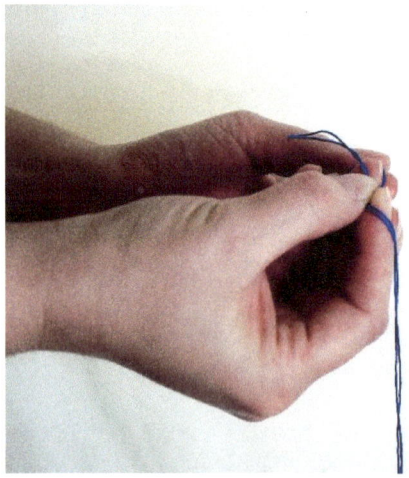

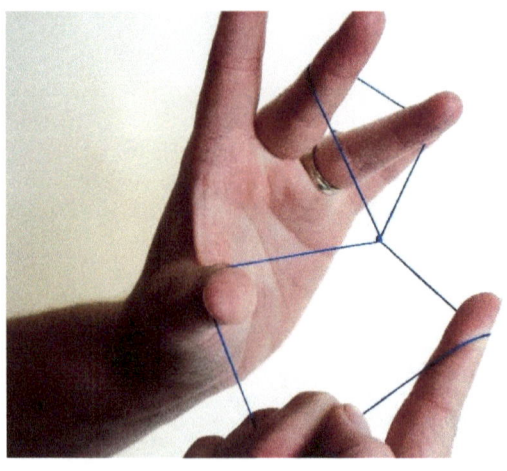

6. Repeat these steps nine more times. Each dangling thread will be wrapped around a single bobbin.

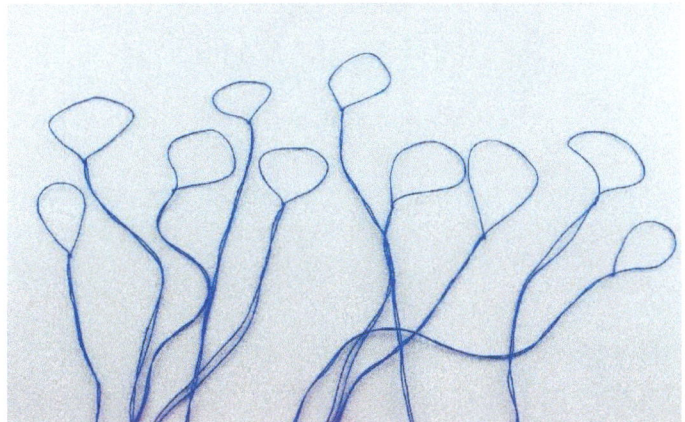

Threading the Bobbins:

1. Take one of the threads and begin to wind it around the neck of the bobbin.

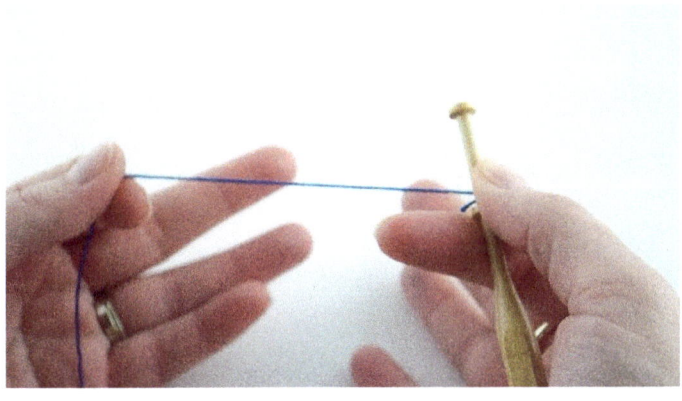

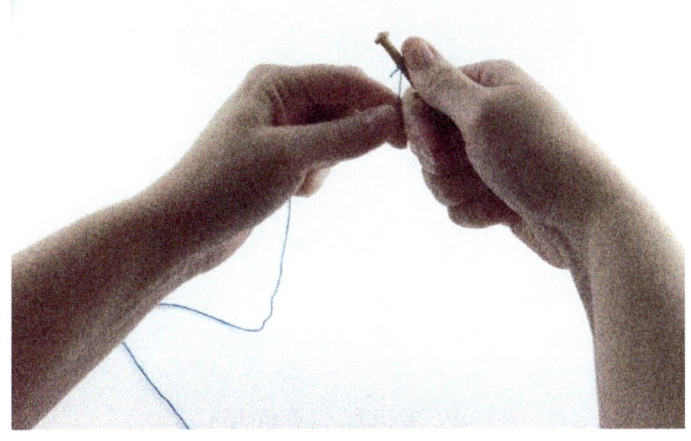

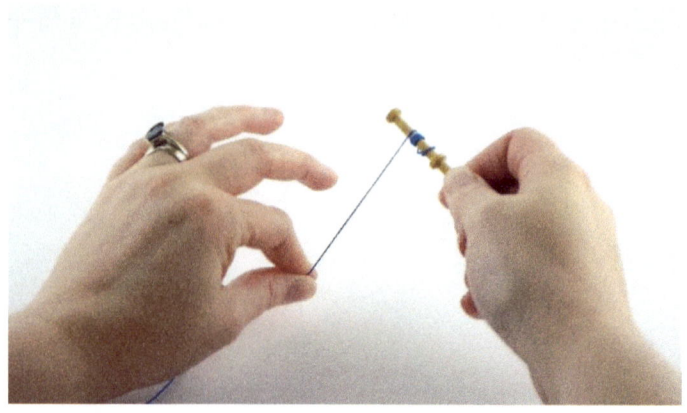

2. Wind the thread until there are 3–4 inches left before the knot.

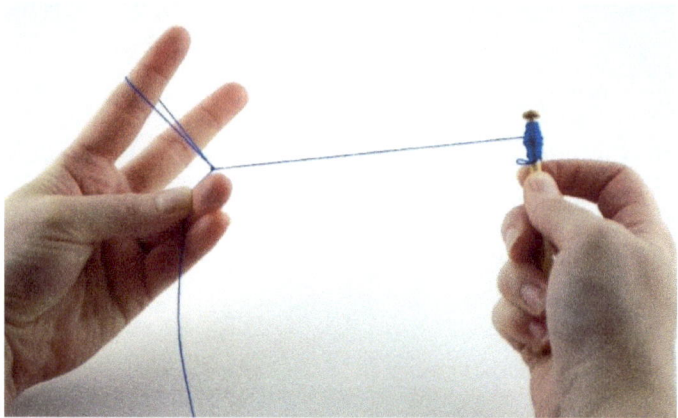

3. Make a simple slip knot and loop it over the top of the bobbin to secure the threads.

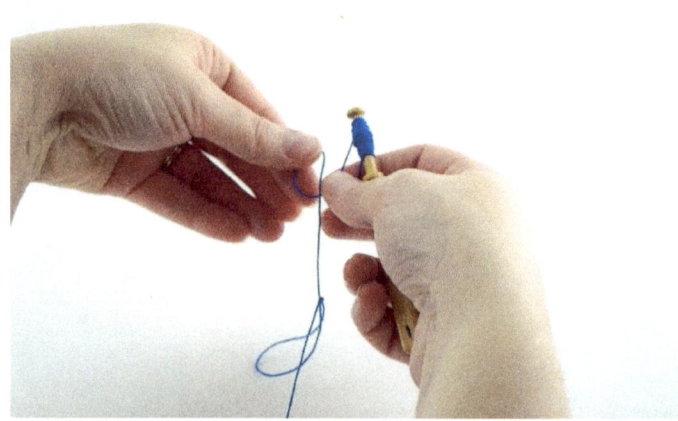

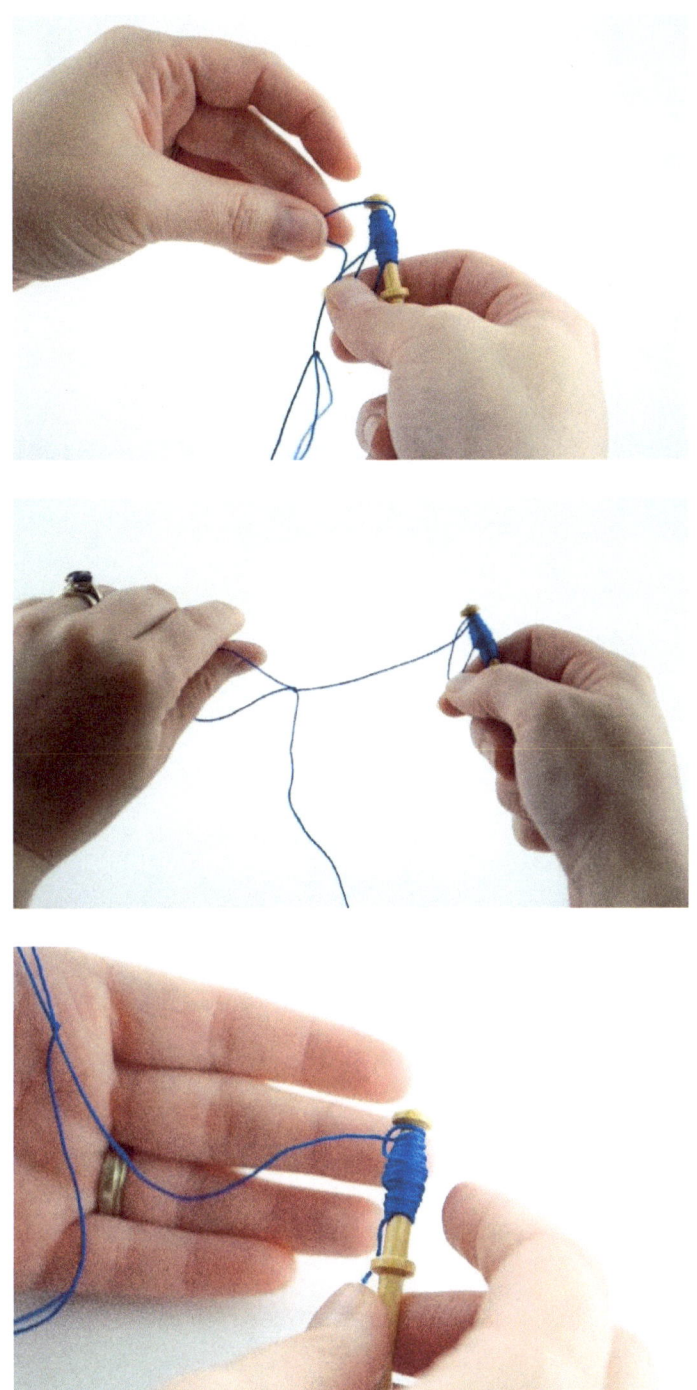

4. Repeat this with a second bobbin with the other thread. Each loop should have two bobbins hanging from it.

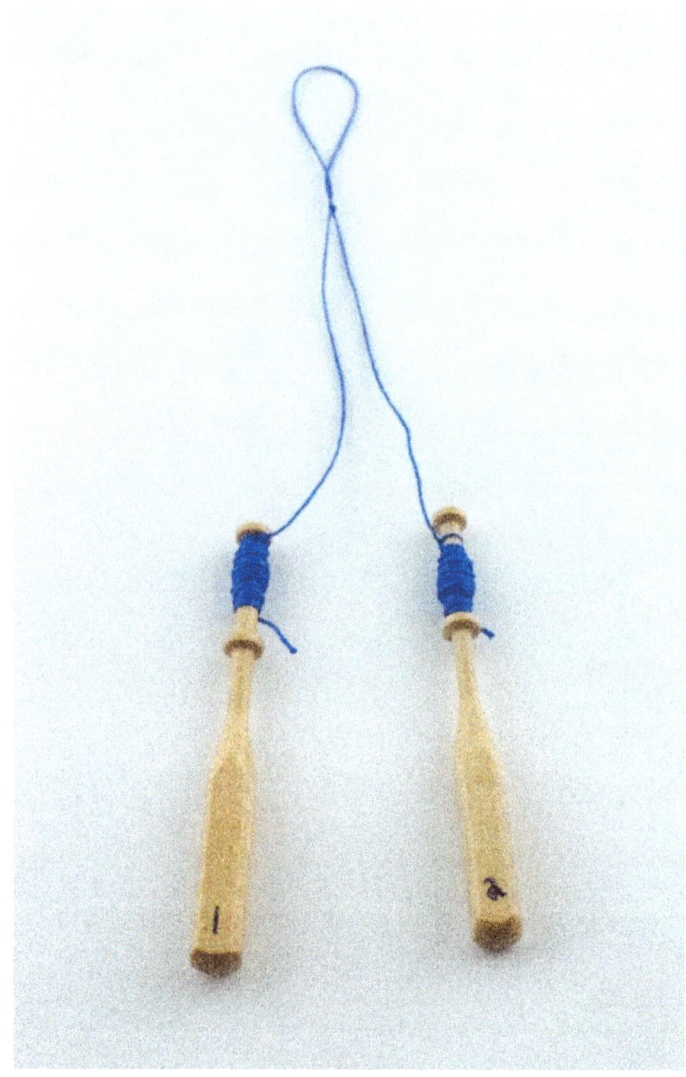

5. Repeat steps 1–4 for the remaining threads and bobbins.

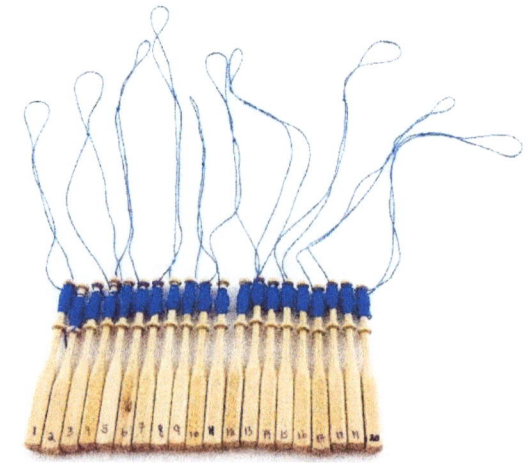

Setting Up Your Pillow:

If you're just starting out with bobbin lace and are unsure about investing in an expensive pillow, I recommend purchasing a small piece of foam board to use for the time being. A stiff throw pillow will also work as a stand-in.

1. Using four pins, center the graph paper pattern in the middle of the pillow or board and pin it down securely at the corners.

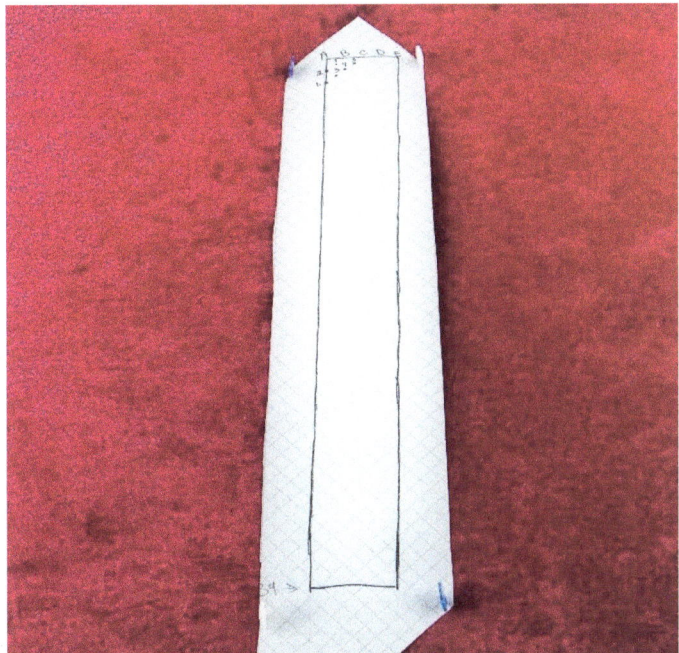

2. Take bobbin sets 1-2 and 3-4 and stick a pin through the knots that make the loops.

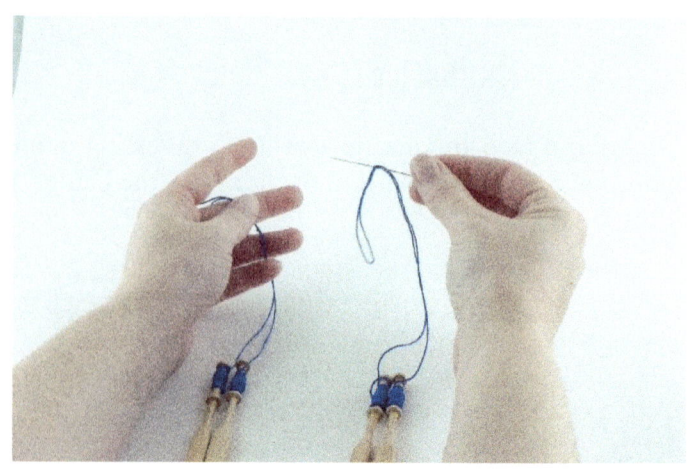

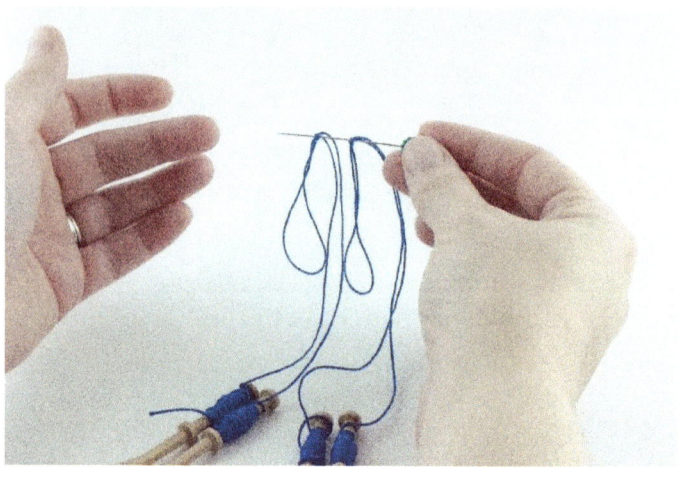

3. Pin the knots at the A dot on the pattern.

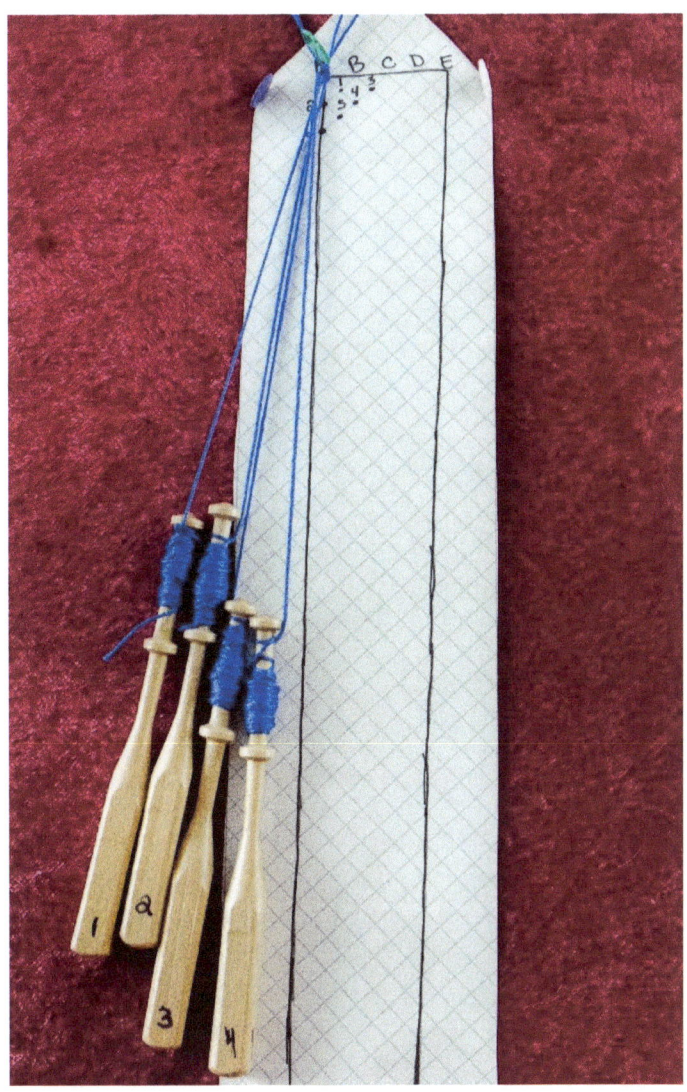

4. Repeat as follows:
   - Pin 5-6 and 7-8 on B dot
   - Pin 9-10 and 11-12 on C dot
   - Pin 13-14 and 15-16 on D dot
   - Pin 17-18 and 19-20 on E dot.

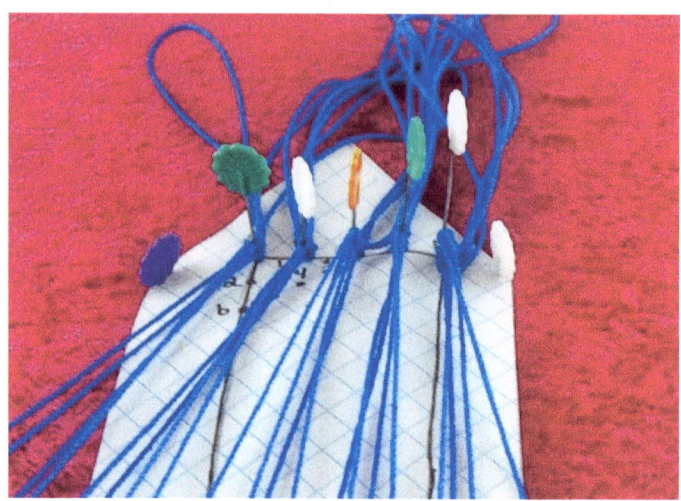

5. To keep the loops from flopping over onto the project, use additional pins to keep them out of the way.

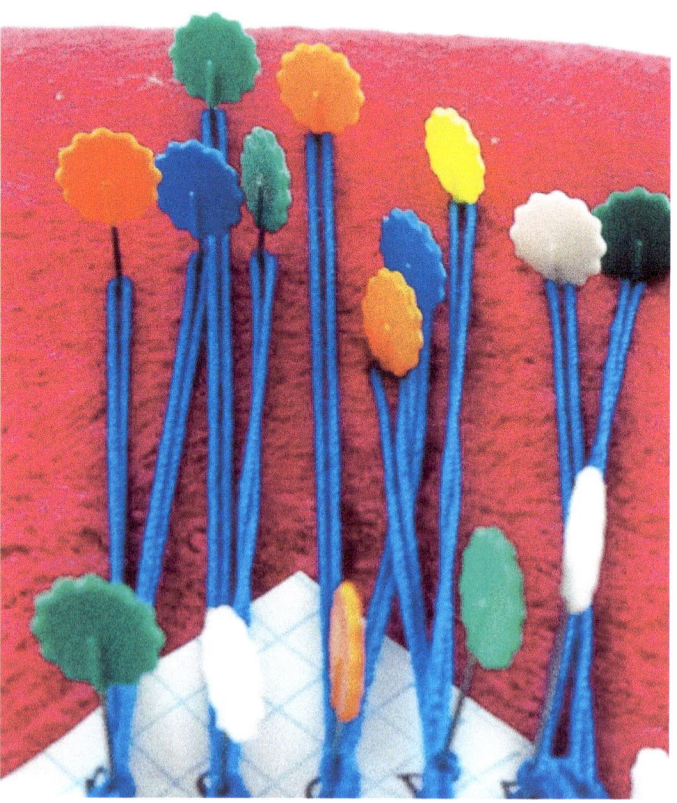

You are now ready to begin the pattern in the next chapter!

Let's Make a Bookmark!

After you've pinned them in place, flip each pair over. Example: Pairs 1-2, 3-4 become 2-1, 4-3.

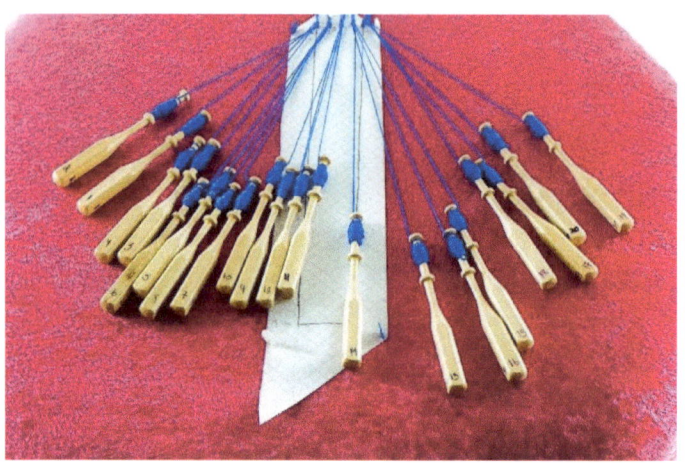

My bobbins are numbered, so the instructions will be referring to numbers.

Common Bobbin Lace Abbreviations	
HST = half-stitch	WST = whole stitch
T = Twist	C = Cross
PR = Pair	PRS = Pairs

When Bobbins Start Unravelling:
    First off, DON'T PANIC! It's going to happen. Slipknots like to undo themselves. Catch it as soon as possible, rewrap the thread around the bobbin, and redo the slipknot. Still happens to me. It's annoying, but not earth shattering.

What Does "Pull" actually mean?
    You're not pulling the threads tight, rather you're gently pulling on the bobbins to slightly tighten the knot you've woven.

What If You Mess Up?
    First off, DON'T PANIC! Simply retrace your steps (or follow the pattern in reverse) until you've corrected your mistake.

Bobbin Pair Order Changes:
    You'll notice was you work through the pattern the bobbin pairs seem to flip order: 6-5 in the first section becomes 5-6 in the second, etc. This is supposed to happen. Trust the system.

One more note: I separate the pins into sets of four to keep things organized and from the twisting together.

Pairs that You're Working With	Instructions
4-3 and 6-5 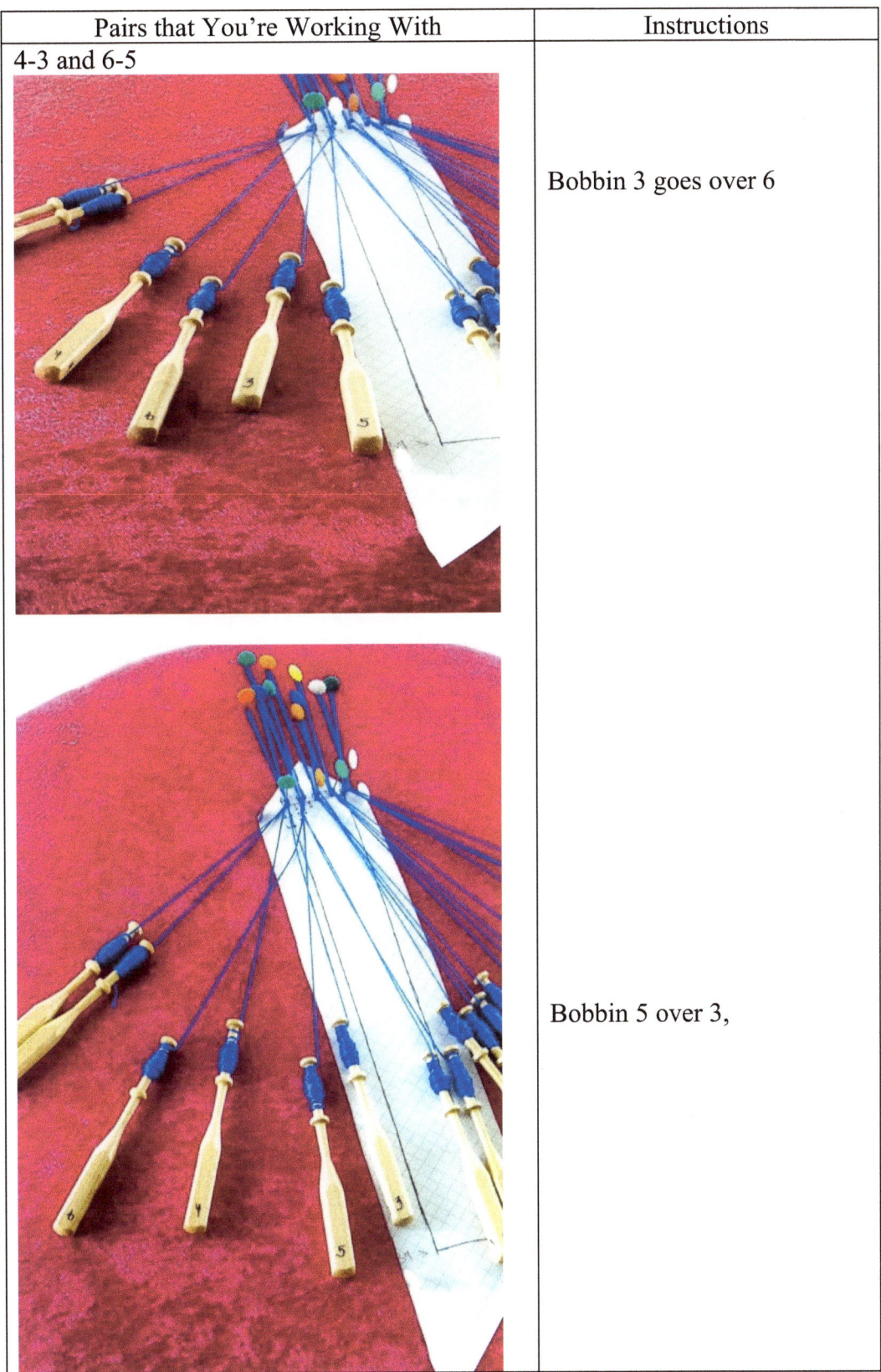	Bobbin 3 goes over 6
	Bobbin 5 over 3,

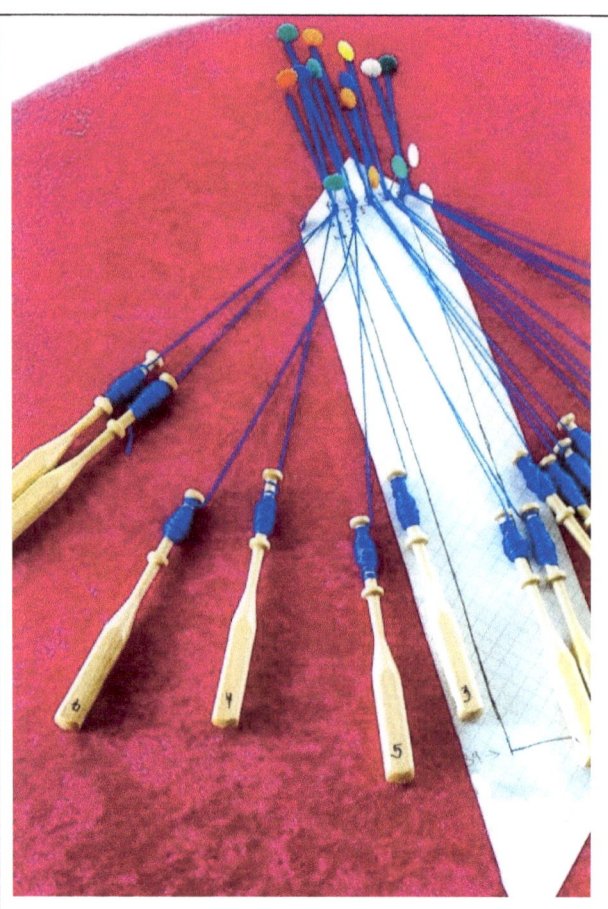

Bobbin 6 over 4,

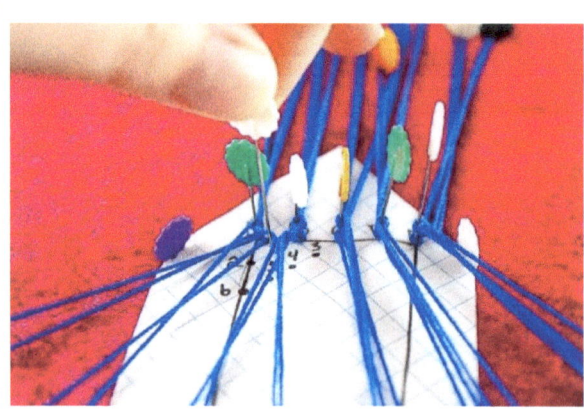

Pin at the apex of where the #1 dot is.

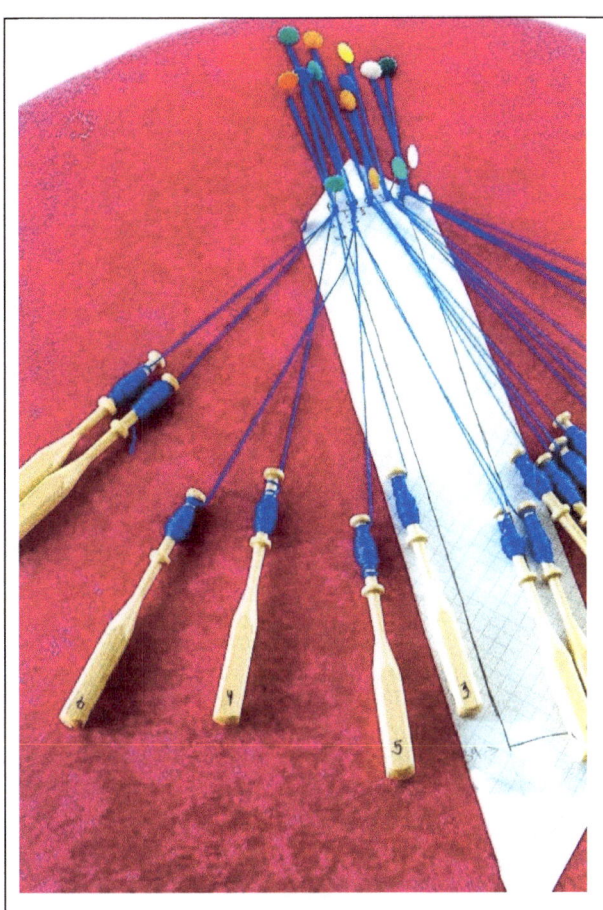

Bobbin 4 over 5,

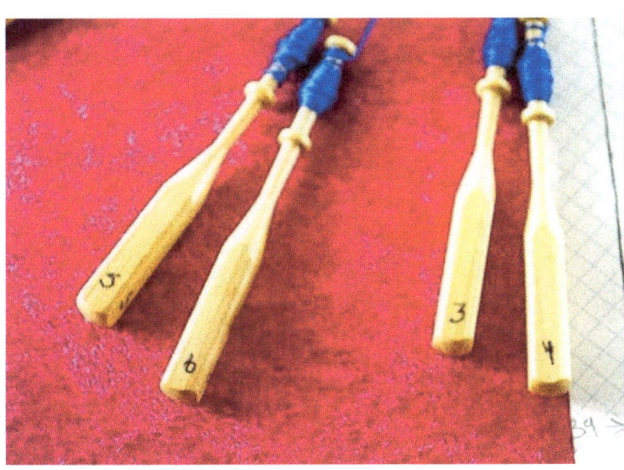

Bobbin 3 over 4,
Bobbin 5 over 6,

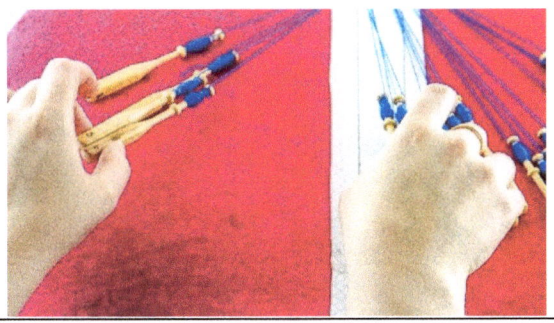

Gently pull the bobbins to tighten the knot.

This is the pattern that will be followed with subsequent pairs.	
2-1 and 5-6	1 over 5 6 over 1 5 over 2 Pin at apex where the #2 dot is. 2 over 6 1 over 2 6 over 5 Pull
8-7 and 10-9	7 over 10 9 over 7 10 over 8 Pin at the apex where the #3 dot is. 8 over 9 7 over 8 9 over 10 Pull
3-4 and 9-10	4 over 9 10 over 4 9 over 3 Pin at the apex where the #4 dot is. 3 over 10 4 over 3 10 over 9

	Pull
1-2 and 10-9	2 over 10
	9 over 2
	10 over 1
	Pin at the apex where the #5 dot is.
	1 over 9
	2 over 1
	9 over 10
	Pull
6-5 and 9-10	5 over 9
	10 over 5
	9 over 6
	Pin at the apex where the #6 dot is.
	6 over 10
	5 over 6
	10 over 9
	Pull
12-11 and 14-13	11 over 14
	13 over 11
	14 over 12
	Pin
	12 over 13
	11 over 12
	13 over 14
	Pull
7-8 and 13-14	8 over 13
	14 over 8
	13 over 7
	Pin
	7 over 14

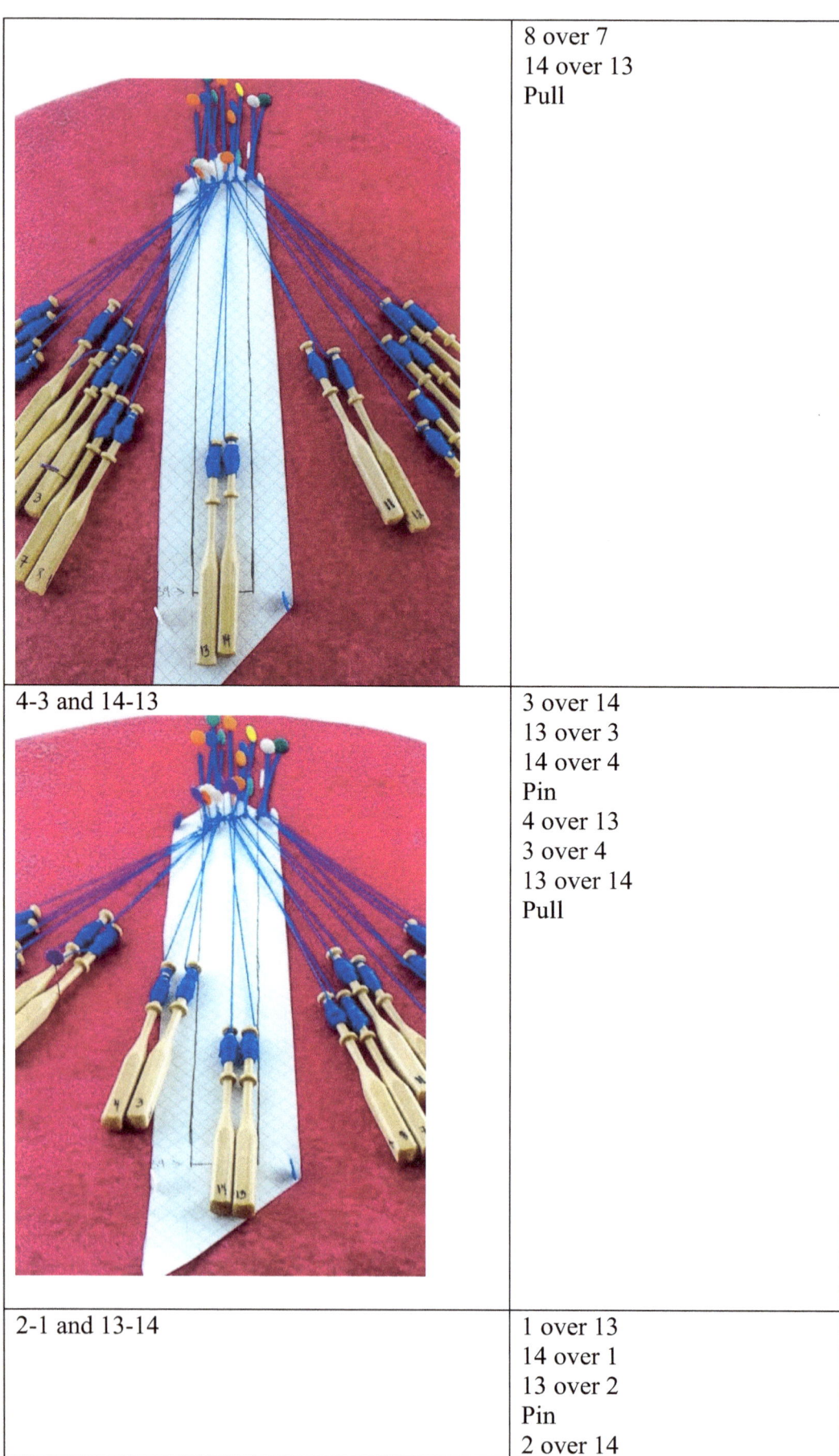	8 over 7 14 over 13 Pull
4-3 and 14-13	3 over 14 13 over 3 14 over 4 Pin 4 over 13 3 over 4 13 over 14 Pull
2-1 and 13-14	1 over 13 14 over 1 13 over 2 Pin 2 over 14

	1 over 2 14 over 13 Pull
5-6 and 14-13	6 over 14 13 over 6 14 over 5 Pin 5 over 13 6 over 5 13 over 14 Pull
10-9 and 13-14	9 over 13 14 over 9 13 over 10 Pin

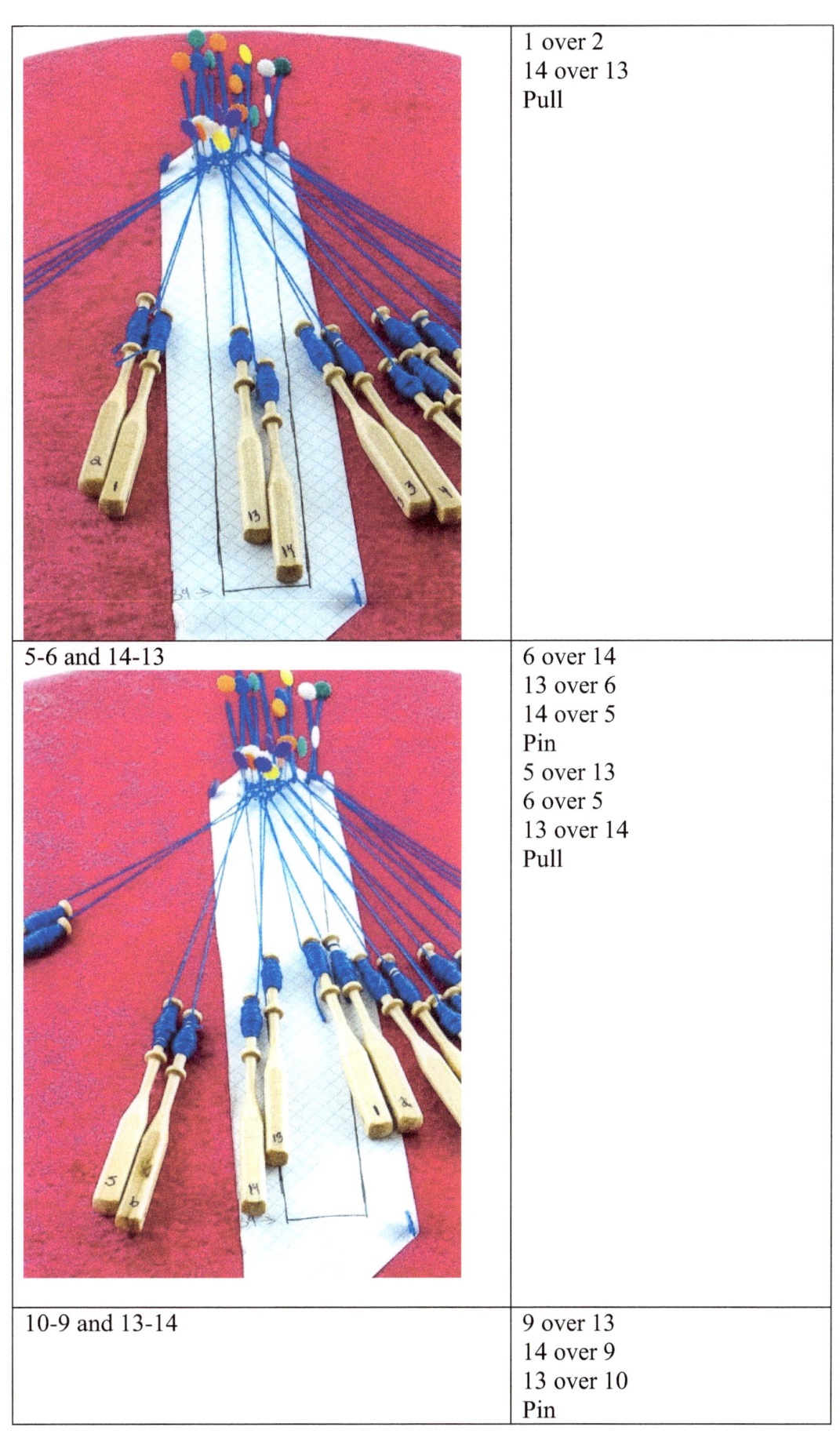

	10 over 14
	9 over 10
	14 over 13
	Pull
16-15 and 18-17	15 over 18
	17 over 15
	18 over 16
	Pin
	16 over 17
	15 over 16
	17 over 18
	Pull
11-12 and 17-18	12 over 17
	18 over 12
	17 over 11
	Pin
	11 over 18
	12 over 11
	18 over 17
	Pull
8-7 and 18-17	7 over 18
	17 over 7
	18 over 8
	Pin
	8 over 17
	7 over 8
	17 over 18
	Pull
3-4 and 17-18	4 over 17
	18 over 4
	17 over 3
	Pin

		3 over 18
		4 over 3
		18 over 17
		Pull
1-2 and 18-17		2 over 18
		17 over 2
		18 over 1
		Pin
		1 over 17
		2 over 1
		17 over 18
		Pull
6-5 and 17-18		5 over 17
		18 over 5
		17 over 6
		Pin
		6 over 18
		5 over 6
		18 over 17
		Pull
9-10 and 18-17		10 over 18
		17 over 10
		18 over 9
		Pin
		9 over 17
		10 over 9
		17 over 18
		Pull
14-13 and 17-18		13 over 17
		18 over 13
		17 over 14
		Pin
		14 over 18
		13 over 14
		18 over 17
		Pull
Starting with the next pair, you will be working through a full row of stitches. You may notice the in each row, one of the pairs you begin with is a pair you work with down the whole row.		
15-16 and 20-19		16 over 20
		19 over 16
		20 over 15
		Pin

	15 over 19
16 over 15
19 over 20
Pull
11-12 and 19-20	11 over 19
20 over 11
19 over 12
Pin
12 over 20
11 over 12
20 over 19
Pull
7-8 and 20-19	8 over 20
19 over 8
20 over 7
Pin
7 over 19
8 over 7
19 over 20
Pull
4-3 and 19-20	3 over 19
20 over 3
19 over 4
Pin
4 over 20
3 over 4
20 over 19
Pull
2-1 and 20-19	1 over 20
19 over 1
20 over 2
Pin
2 over 19
1 over 2
19 over 20
Pull
5-6 and 19-20	6 over 19
20 over 6
19 over 5
Pin
5 over 20
6 over 5
20 over 19
Pull
10-9 and 20-19	9 over 20
19 over 9
20 over 10
Pin

	10 over 19
	9 over 10
	19 over 20
	Pull
13-14 and 19-20	14 over 19
	20 over 14
	19 over 13
	Pin
	13 over 20
	14 over 13
	20 over 19
	Pull
17-18 and 20-19	17 over 20
	19 over 17
	20 over 18
	Pin
	18 over 19
	17 over 18
	19 over 20
	Pull

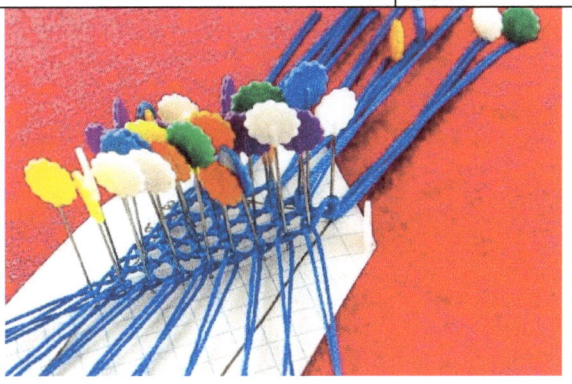

Pins should be in this order: 19-20; 17-18; 14-13; 9-10; 6-5; 1-2; 3-4; 8-7; 11-12; 16-15

You may find it easier to turn the pillow as you work through the bobbins.

NEW ROW! 11-12 and 16-15	12 over 16
	15 over 12
	16 over 11
	Pin
	11 over 15
	12 over 11
	15 over 16
	Pull
8-7 and 15-16	7 over 15
	16 over 7
	15 over 8

	Pin 8 over 16 7 over 8 16 over 15 Pull
3-4 and 16-15	4 over 16 15 over 4 16 over 3 Pin 3 over 15 4 over 3 15 over 16 Pull
1-2 and 15-16	2 over 15 16 over 2 15 over 1 Pin 1 over 16 2 over 1 16 over 15 Pull
6-5 and 16-15	5 over 16 15 over 5 16 over 6 Pin 6 over 15 5 over 6 15 over 16 Pull
9-10 and 15-16	10 over 15 16 over 10 15 over 9 Pin 9 over 16 10 over 9 16 over 15 Pull
14-13 and 16-15	13 over 16 15 over 13 16 over 14 Pin 14 over 15 13 over 14 15 over 16 Pull
17-18 and 15-16	18 over 15 16 over 18 15 over 17

	Pin
	17 over 16
	18 over 17
	16 over 15
	Pull
19-20 and 16-15	20 over 16
	15 over 20
	16 over 19
	Pin
	19 over 15
	20 over 19
	15 over 16
	Pull

Congratulations! You just completed a full row of bobbin lace! If you need to stop for the day, I recommend stopping at a finished row. It's easier to keep bobbins from getting mixed up.

NEW ROW! 7-8 and 12-11	8 over 12
	11 over 8
	12 over 7
	Pin
	7 over 11
	8 over 7
	11 over 12
	Pull
4-3 and 11-12	3 over 11
	12 over 3
	11 over 4
	Pin
	4 over 12
	3 over 4
	12 over 11
	Pull
2-1 and 12-11	1 over 12
	11 over 1
	12 over 2
	Pin
	2 over 11
	1 over 2
	11 over 12
	Pull
5-6 and 11-12	6 over 11
	12 over 6
	11 over 5

	Pin 5 over 12 6 over 5 12 over 11 Pull
10-9 and 12-11	9 over 12 11 over 9 12 over 10 Pin 10 over 11 9 over 10 11 over 12 Pull
13-14 and 11-12	14 over 11 12 over 14 11 over 13 Pin 13 over 12 14 over 13 12 over 11 Pull
18-17 and 12-11	17 over 12 11 over 17 12 over 18 Pin 18 over 11 17 over 18 11 over 12 Pull
20-19 and 11-12	19 over 11 12 over 19 11 over 20 Pin 20 over 12 19 over 20 12 over 11 Pull
15-16 and 12-11	16 over 12 11 over 16 12 over 15 Pin 15 over 11 16 over 15 11 over 12 Pull
NEW ROW! 3-4 and 8-7	4 over 8 7 over 4 8 over 3

	Pin
	3 over 7
	4 over 3
	7 over 8
	Pull
1-2 and 7-8	2 over 7
	8 over 2
	7 over 1
	Pin
	1 over 8
	2 over 1
	8 over 7
	Pull
6-5 and 8-7	5 over 8
	7 over 5
	8 over 6
	Pin
	6 over 7
	5 over 6
	7 over 8
	Pull
9-10 and 7-8	10 over 7
	8 over 10
	7 over 9
	Pin
	9 over 8
	10 over 9
	8 over 7
	Pull
14-13 and 8-7	13 over 8
	7 over 13
	8 over 14
	Pin
	14 over 7
	13 over 14
	7 over 8
	Pull
17-18 and 7-8	18 over 7
	8 over 18
	7 over 17
	Pin
	17 over 8
	18 over 17
	8 over 7
	Pull
19-20 and 8-7	20 over 8
	7 over 20
	8 over 19

	Pin 19 over 7 20 over 19 7 over 8 Pull
16-15 and 7-8	15 over 7 8 over 15 7 over 16 Pin 16 over 8 15 over 16 8 over 7 Pull
11-12 and 8-7	12 over 8 7 over 12 8 over 11 Pin 11 over 7 12 over 11 7 over 8 Pull
NEW ROW! 2-1 and 4-3	1 over 4 3 over 1 4 over 2 Pin 2 over 3 1 over 2 3 over 4 Pull
5-6 and 3-4	6 over 3 4 over 6 3 over 5 Pin 5 over 4 6 over 5 4 over 3 Pull
10-9 and 4-3	9 over 4 3 over 9 4 over 10 Pin 10 over 3 9 over 10 3 over 4 Pull
13-14 and 3-4	14 over 3 4 over 14 3 over 13

	Pin 13 over 4 14 over 13 4 over 3 Pull
18-17 and 4-3	17 over 4 3 over 17 4 over 18 Pin 18 over 3 17 over 18 3 over 4 Pull
20-19 and 3-4	19 over 3 4 over 19 3 over 20 Pin 20 over 4 19 over 20 4 over 3 Pull
15-16 and 4-3	16 over 4 3 over 16 4 over 15 Pin 15 over 3 16 over 15 3 over 4 Pull
12-11 and 3-4	11 over 3 4 over 11 3 over 12 Pin 12 over 4 11 over 12 4 over 3 Pull
7-8 and 4-3	8 over 4 3 over 8 4 over 7 Pin 7 over 3 8 over 7 3 over 4 Pull

Pins should be in this order: 3-4; 8-7; 11-12; 16-15; 19-20; 17-18; 14-13; 9-10; 6-5; 1-2

NEW ROW! 6-5 and 1-2	5 over 1 2 over 5 1 over 6 Pin 6 over 2 5 over 6 2 over 1 Pull
9-10 and 2-1	10 over 2 1 over 10 2 over 9 Pin 9 over 1 10 over 9 1 over 2 Pull
14-13 and 1-2	13 over 1 2 over 13 1 over 14 Pin 14 over 2 13 over 14 2 over 1 Pull
17-18 and 2-1	18 over 2 1 over 18 2 over 17 Pin 17 over 1 18 over 17 1 over 2 Pull

19-20 and 1-2	20 over 1 2 over 20 1 over 19 Pin 19 over 2 20 over 19 2 over 1 Pull
16-15 and 2-1	15 over 2 1 over 15 2 over 16 Pin 16 over 1 15 over 16 1 over 2 Pull
11-12 and 1-2	12 over 1 2 over 12 1 over 11 Pin 11 over 2 12 over 11 2 over 1 Pull
8-7 and 2-1	7 over 2 1 over 7 2 over 8 Pin 8 over 1 7 over 8 1 over 2 Pull
3-4 and 1-2	4 over 1 2 over 4 1 over 3 Pin 3 over 2 4 over 3 2 over 1 Pull
NEW ROW! 10-9 and 5-6	9 over 5 6 over 9 5 over 10 Pin 10 over 6 9 over 10 6 over 5 Pull

13-14 and 6-5	14 over 6 5 over 14 6 over 13 Pin 13 over 5 14 over 13 5 over 6 Pull
18-17 and 5-6	17 over 5 6 over 17 5 over 18 Pin 18 over 6 17 over 18 6 over 5 Pull
20-19 and 6-5	19 over 6 5 over 19 6 over 20 Pin 20 over 5 19 over 20 5 over 6 Pull
15-16 and 5-6	16 over 5 6 over 16 5 over 15 Pin 15 over 6 16 over 15 6 over 5 Pull
12-11 and 6-5	11 over 6 5 over 11 6 over 12 Pin 12 over 5 11 over 12 5 over 6 Pull
7-8 and 5-6	8 over 5 6 over 8 5 over 7 Pin 7 over 6 8 over 7 6 over 5 Pull

4-3 and 6-5	3 over 6 5 over 3 6 over 4 Pin 4 over 5 3 over 4 5 over 6 Pull
2-1 and 5-6	1 over 5 6 over 1 5 over 2 Pin 2 over 6 1 over 2 6 over 5 Pull
New Row! 14-13 and 9-10	13 over 9 10 over 13 9 over 14 Pin 14 over 10 13 over 14 10 over 9 Pull
17-18 and 10-9	18 over 10 9 over 18 10 over 17 Pin 17 over 9 18 over 17 9 over 10 Pull
19-20 and 9-10	20 over 9 10 over 20 9 over 19 Pin 10 over 19 20 over 10 19 over 9 Pull
16-15 and 10-9	15 over 10 9 over 15 10 over 16 Pin 16 over 9 15 over 16 9 over 10 Pull

11-12 and 9-10	12 over 9 10 over 12 9 over 11 Pin 11 over 10 12 over 11 10 over 9 Pull
8-7 and 10-9	7 over 10 9 over 7 10 over 8 Pin 8 over 9 7 over 8 9 over 10 Pull
3-4 and 9-10	4 over 9 10 over 4 9 over 3 Pin 3 over 10 4 over 3 10 over 9 Pull
1-2 and 10-9	2 over 10 9 over 2 10 over 1 Pin 1 over 9 2 over 1 9 over 10 Pull
6-5 and 9-10	5 over 9 10 over 5 9 over 6 Pin 6 over 10 5 over 6 10 over 9 Pull

Pins should be in this order: 10-9; 6-5; 2-1; 4-3; 7-8; 12-11; 15-16; 20-19; 18-17; 13-14

New Row! 18-17 and 13-14	17 over 13 14 over 17 13 over 18 Pin 18 over 14 17 over 18 14 over 13 Pull
20-19 and 14-13	19 over 14 13 over 19 14 over 20 Pin 20 over 13 19 over 20 13 over 14 Pull
15-16 and 13-14	16 over 13 14 over 16 13 over 15 Pin 15 over 14 16 over 15 14 over 13

	Pull
12-11 and 14-13	11 over 14 13 over 11 14 over 12 Pin 12 over 13 11 over 12 13 over 14 Pull
7-8 and 13-14	8 over 13 14 over 8 13 over 7 Pin 7 over 14 8 over 7 14 over 13 Pull
4-3 and 14-13	3 over 14 13 over 3 14 over 4 Pin 4 over 13 3 over 4 13 over 14 Pull
2-1 and 13-14	1 over 13 14 over 1 13 over 2 Pin 2 over 14 1 over 2 14 over 13 Pull
5-6 and 14-13	6 over 14 13 over 6 14 over 5 Pin 5 over 13 6 over 5 13 over 14 Pull
10-9 and 13-14	9 over 13 14 over 9 13 over 10 Pin 10 over 14 9 over 10 14 over 13

	Pull
NEW ROW! 19-20 and 17-18	20 over 17 18 over 20 17 over 19 Pin 19 over 18 20 over 19 18 over 17 Pull
16-15 and 18-17	15 over 18 17 over 15 18 over 16 Pin 16 over 17 15 over 16 17 over 18 Pull
11-12 and 17-18	12 over 17 18 over 12 17 over 11 Pin 11 over 18 12 over 11 18 over 17 Pull
8-7 and 18-17	7 over 18 17 over 7 18 over 8 Pin 8 over 17 7 over 8 17 over 18 Pull
3-4 and 17-18	4 over 17 18 over 4 17 over 3 Pin 3 over 18 4 over 3 18 over 17 Pull
1-2 and 18-17	2 over 18 17 over 2 18 over 1 Pin 1 over 17 2 over 1 17 over 18

	Pull
6-5 and 17-18	5 over 17
	18 over 5
	17 over 6
	Pin
	6 over 18
	5 over 6
	18 over 17
	Pull
9-10 and 18-17	10 over 18
	17 over 10
	18 over 9
	Pin
	9 over 17
	10 over 9
	17 over 18
	Pull
14-13 and 17-18	13 over 17
	18 over 13
	17 over 14
	Pin
	14 over 18
	13 over 14
	18 over 17
	Pull
NEW ROW! 15-16 and 20-19	16 over 20
	19 over 16
	20 over 15
	Pin
	15 over 19
	16 over 15
	19 over 20
	Pull
12-11 and 19-20	11 over 19
	20 over 11
	19 over 12
	Pin
	12 over 20
	11 over 12
	20 over 19
	Pull
7-8 and 20-19	8 over 20
	19 over 8
	20 over 7
	Pin
	7 over 19
	8 over 7
	19 over 20

	Pull
4-3 and 19-20	3 over 19
	20 over 3
	19 over 4
	Pin
	4 over 20
	3 over 4
	20 over 19
	Pull
2-1 20-19	1 over 20
	19 over 1
	20 over 2
	Pin
	2 over 19
	1 over 2
	19 over 20
	Pull
5-6 and 19-20	6 over 19
	20 over 6
	19 over 5
	Pin
	5 over 20
	6 over 5
	20 over 19
	Pull
10-9 and 20-19	9 over 20
	19 over 9
	20 over 10
	Pin
	10 over 19
	9 over 10
	19 over 20
	Pull
13-14 and 19-20	14 over 19
	20 over 14
	19 over 13
	Pin
	13 over 20
	14 over 13
	20 over 19
	Pull
18-17 and 20-19	17 over 20
	19 over 17
	20 over 18
	Pin
	18 over 19
	17 over 18
	19 over 20

	Pull
NEW ROW! 11-12 and 16-15	12 over 16 15 over 12 16 over 11 Pin 11 over 15 12 over 11 15 over 16 Pull
8-7 and 15-16	7 over 15 16 over 7 15 over 8 Pin 8 over 16 7 over 8 16 over 15 Pull
3-4 and 16-15	4 over 16 15 over 4 16 over 3 Pin 3 over 15 4 over 3 15 over 16 Pull
1-2 and 15-16	2 over 15 16 over 2 15 over 1 Pin 1 over 16 2 over 1 16 over 15 Pull
6-5 and 16-15	5 over 16 15 over 5 16 over 6 Pin 6 over 15 5 over 6 15 over 16 Pull
9-10 and 15-16	10 over 15 16 over 10 15 over 9 Pin 9 over 16 10 over 9 16 over 15

	Pull
14-13 and 16-15	13 over 16
	15 over 13
	16 over 14
	Pin
	14 over 15
	13 over 14
	15 over 16
	Pull
17-18 and 15-16	18 over 15
	16 over 18
	15 over 17
	Pin
	17 over 16
	18 over 17
	16 over 15
	Pull
19-20 and 16-15	20 over 16
	15 over 20
	16 over 19
	Pin
	19 over 15
	20 over 19
	15 over 16
	Pull

Pins should be in this order: 15-16; 20-19; 18-17; 13-14; 10-9; 5-6; 2-1; 4-3; 7-8; 12-11	
NEW ROW! 7-8 and 12-11	8 over 12 11 over 8 12 over 7 Pin 7 over 11 8 over 7 11 over 12 Pull
4-3 and 11-12	3 over 11 12 over 3 11 over 4 Pin 4 over 12 3 over 4 12 over 11 Pull
2-1 and 12-11	1 over 12 11 over 1 12 over 2 Pin 2 over 11 1 over 2 11 over 12 Pull
5-6 and 11-12	6 over 11 12 over 6 11 over 5 Pin 5 over 12 6 over 5 12 over 11 Pull
10-9 and 12-11	9 over 12 11 over 9 12 over 10 Pin 10 over 11 9 over 10 11 over 12 Pull
13-14 and 11-12	14 over 11 12 over 14 11 over 13 Pin 13 over 12 14 over 13

	12 over 11 Pull
18-17 and 12-11	17 over 12 11 over 17 12 over 18 Pin 18 over 11 17 over 18 11 over 12 Pull
20-19 and 11-12	19 over 11 12 over 19 11 over 20 Pin 20 over 12 19 over 20 12 over 11 Pull
15-16 and 12-11	16 over 12 11 over 16 12 over 15 Pin 15 over 11 16 over 15 11 over 12 Pull
NEW ROW! 3-4 and 8-7	4 over 8 7 over 4 8 over 3 Pin 3 over 7 4 over 3 7 over 8 Pull
1-2 and 7-8	2 over 7 8 over 2 7 over 1 Pin 1 over 8 2 over 1 8 over 7 Pull
6-5 and 8-7	5 over 8 7 over 5 8 over 6 Pin 6 over 7 5 over 6

	7 over 8 Pull
9-10 and 7-8	10 over 7 8 over 10 7 over 9 Pin 9 over 8 10 over 9 8 over 7 Pull
14-13 and 8-7	13 over 8 7 over 13 8 over 14 Pin 14 over 7 13 over 14 7 over 8 Pull
17-18 and 7-8	18 over 7 8 over 18 7 over 17 Pin 17 over 8 18 over 17 8 over 7 Pull
19-20 and 8-7	20 over 8 7 over 20 8 over 19 Pin 19 over 7 20 over 19 7 over 8 Pull
16-15 and 7-8	15 over 7 8 over 15 7 over 16 Pin 16 over 8 15 over 16 8 over 7 Pull
11-12 and 8-7	12 over 8 7 over 12 8 over 11 Pin 11 over 7 12 over 11

	7 over 8
	Pull
NEW ROW! 2-1 and 4-3	1 over 4
	3 over 1
	4 over 2
	Pin
	2 over 3
	1 over 2
	3 over 4
	Pull
5-6 and 3-4	6 over 3
	4 over 6
	3 over 5
	Pin
	5 over 4
	6 over 5
	4 over 3
	Pull
10-9 and 4-3	9 over 4
	3 over 9
	4 over 10
	Pin
	10 over 3
	9 over 10
	3 over 4
	Pull
13-14 and 3-4	14 over 3
	4 over 14
	3 over 13
	Pin
	13 over 4
	14 over 13
	4 over 3
	Pull
18-17 and 4-3	17 over 4
	3 over 17
	4 over 18
	Pin
	18 over 3
	17 over 18
	3 over 4
	Pull
20-19 and 3-4	19 over 3
	4 over 19
	3 over 20
	Pin
	20 over 4
	19 over 20

| | 4 over 3
Pull |
| 15-16 and 4-3 | 16 over 4
3 over 16
4 over 15
Pin
15 over 3
16 over 15
3 over 4
Pull |
| 12-11 and 3-4 | 11 over 3
4 over 11
3 over 12
Pin
12 over 4
11 over 12
4 over 3
Pull |
| 7-8 and 4-3 | 8 over 4
3 over 8
4 over 7
Pin
7 over 3
8 over 7
3 over 4
Pull |
| NEW ROW!
6-5 and 1-2 | 5 over 1
2 over 5
1 over 6
Pin
6 over 2
5 over 6
2 over 1
Pull |
| 9-10 and 2-1 | 10 over 2
1 over 10
2 over 9
Pin
9 over 1
10 over 9
1 over 2
Pull |
| 14-13 and 1-2 | 13 over 1
2 over 13
1 over 14
Pin
14 over 2
13 over 14 |

	2 over 1
	Pull
17-18 and 2-1	18 over 2
	1 over 18
	2 over 17
	Pin
	17 over 1
	18 over 17
	1 over 2
	Pull
19-20 and 1-2	20 over 1
	2 over 20
	1 over 19
	Pin
	19 over 2
	20 over 19
	2 over 1
	Pull
16-15 and 2-1	15 over 2
	1 over 15
	2 over 16
	Pin
	16 over 1
	15 over 16
	1 over 2
	Pull
11-12 and 1-2	12 over 1
	2 over 12
	1 over 11
	Pin
	11 over 2
	12 over 11
	2 over 1
	Pull
8-7 and 2-1	7 over 2
	1 over 7
	2 over 8
	Pin
	8 over 1
	7 over 8
	1 over 2
	Pull
3-4 and 1-2 Pins should be in this order: 2-1; 3-4; 7-8; 12-11; 15-16; 20-19; 18-17; 13-14; 10-9; 5-6	4 over 1
	2 over 4
	1 over 3
	Pin
	3 over 2
	4 over 3

	2 over 1 Pull
NEW ROW! 10-9 and 5-6	9 over 5 6 over 9 5 over 10 Pin 10 over 6 9 over 10 6 over 5 Pull
13-14 and 6-5	14 over 6 5 over 14 6 over 13 Pin 13 over 5 14 over 13 5 over 6 Pull
18-17 and 5-6	17 over 5 6 over 17 5 over 18 Pin 18 over 6 17 over 18 6 over 5 Pull
20-19 and 6-5	19 over 6 5 over 19 6 over 20 Pin 20 over 5 19 over 20 5 over 6 Pull
15-16 and 5-6	16 over 5 6 over 16 5 over 15 Pin 15 over 6 16 over 15 6 over 5 Pull
12-11 and 6-5	11 over 6 5 over 11 6 over 12 Pin 12 over 5 11 over 12

	5 over 6 Pull
7-8 and 5-6	8 over 5 6 over 8 5 over 7 Pin 7 over 6 8 over 7 6 over 5 Pull
4-3 and 6-5	3 over 6 5 over 3 6 over 4 Pin 4 over 5 3 over 4 5 over 6 Pull
2-1 and 5-6	1 over 5 6 over 1 5 over 2 Pin 2 over 6 1 over 2 6 over 5 Pull
NEW ROW! 14-13 and 9-10	13 over 9 10 over 13 9 over 14 Pin 14 over 10 13 over 14 10 over 9 Pull
17-18 and 10-9	18 over 10 9 over 18 10 over 17 Pin 17 over 9 18 over 17 9 over 10 Pull
19-20 and 9-10	20 over 9 10 over 20 9 over 19 Pin 19 over 10 20 over 19

	10 over 9 Pull
16-15 and 10-9	15 over 10 9 over 15 10 over 16 Pin 16 over 9 15 over 16 9 over 10 Pull
11-12 and 9-10	12 over 9 10 over 12 9 over 11 Pin 11 over 10 12 over 11 10 over 9 Pull
8-7 and 10-9	7 over 10 9 over 7 10 over 8 Pin 8 over 9 7 over 8 9 over 10 Pull
3-4 and 9-10	4 over 9 10 over 4 9 over 3 Pin 3 over 10 4 over 3 10 over 9 Pull
1-2 and 10-9	2 over 10 9 over 2 10 over 1 Pin 1 over 9 2 over 1 9 over 10 Pull
6-5 and 9-10	5 over 9 10 over 5 9 over 6 Pin 6 over 10 5 over 6

	10 over 9
	Pull
NEW ROW! 18-17 and 13-14	17 over 13
	14 over 17
	13 over 18
	Pin
	18 over 14
	17 over 18
	14 over 13
	Pull
20-19 and 14-13	19 over 14
	13 over 19
	14 over 20
	Pin
	20 over 13
	19 over 20
	13 over 14
	Pull
15-16 and 13-14	16 over 13
	14 over 16
	13 over 15
	Pin
	15 over 14
	16 over 15
	14 over 13
	Pull
12-11 and 14-13	11 over 14
	13 over 11
	14 over 12
	Pin
	12 over 13
	11 over 12
	13 over 14
	Pull
7-8 and 13-14	8 over 13
	14 over 8
	13 over 7
	Pin
	7 over 14
	8 over 7
	14 over 13
	Pull
4-3 and 14-13	3 over 14
	13 over 3
	14 over 4
	Pin
	4 over 13
	3 over 4

	13 over 14 Pull
2-1 and 13-14	1 over 13 14 over 1 13 over 2 Pin 2 over 14 1 over 2 14 over 13 Pull
5-6 and 14-13	6 over 14 13 over 6 14 over 5 Pin 5 over 13 6 over 5 13 over 14 Pull
10-9 and 13-14	9 over 13 14 over 9 13 over 10 Pin 10 over 14 9 over 10 14 over 13 Pull
NEW ROW! 19-20 and 17-18	20 over 17 18 over 20 17 over 19 Pin 19 over 18 20 over 19 18 over 17 Pull
16-15 and 18-17	15 over 18 17 over 15 18 over 16 Pin 16 over 17 15 over 16 17 over 18 Pull
11-12 and 17-18	12 over 17 18 over 12 17 over 11 Pin 11 over 18 12 over 11

	18 over 17 Pull
8-7 and 18-17	7 over 18 17 over 7 18 over 8 Pin 8 over 17 7 over 8 17 over 18 Pull
3-4 and 17-18	4 over 17 18 over 4 17 over 3 Pin 3 over 18 4 over 3 18 over 17 Pull
1-2 and 18-17	2 over 18 17 over 2 18 over 1 Pin 1 over 17 2 over 1 17 over 18 Pull
6-5 and 17-18	5 over 17 18 over 5 17 over 6 Pin 6 over 18 5 over 6 18 over 17 Pull
9-10 and 18-17	10 over 18 17 over 10 18 over 9 Pin 9 over 17 10 over 9 17 over 18 Pull
14-13 and 17-18 Pins should be in this order: 18-17; 13-14; 10-9; 5-6; 2-1; 4-3; 7-8; 12-11; 15-16; 20-19	13 over 17 18 over 13 17 over 14 Pin 14 over 18 13 over 14

	18 over 17 Pull
NEW ROW!!! 15-16 and 20-19	16 over 20 19 over 16 20 over 15 Pin 15 over 19 16 over 15 19 over 20 Pull
12-11 and 19-20	11 over 19 20 over 11 19 over 12 Pin 12 over 20 11 over 12 20 over 19 Pull
7-8 and 20-19	8 over 20 19 over 8 20 over 7 Pin 7 over 19 8 over 7 19 over 20 Pull
4-3 and 19-20	3 over 19 20 over 3 19 over 4 Pin 4 over 20 3 over 4 20 over 19 Pull
2-1 and 20-19	1 over 20 19 over 1 20 over 2 Pin 2 over 19 1 over 2 19 over 20 Pull
5-6 and 19-20	6 over 19 20 over 6 19 over 5 Pin 5 over 20 6 over 5

	20 over 19 Pull
10-9 and 20-19	9 over 20 19 over 9 20 over 10 Pin 10 over 19 9 over 10 19 over 20 Pull
13-14 and 19-20	14 over 19 20 over 14 19 over 13 Pin 13 over 20 14 over 13 20 over 19 Pull
18-17 and 20-19	17 over 20 19 over 17 20 over 18 Pin 18 over 19 17 over 18 19 over 20 Pull
NEW ROW!!! 11-12 and 16-15	12 over 16 15 over 12 16 over 11 Pin 11 over 15 12 over 11 15 over 16 Pull
8-7 and 15-16	7 over 15 16 over 7 15 over 8 Pin 8 over 16 7 over 8 16 over 15 Pull
3-4 and 16-15	4 over 16 15 over 4 16 over 3 Pin 3 over 15 4 over 3

	15 over 16 Pull
1-2 and 15-16	2 over 15 16 over 2 15 over 1 Pin 1 over 16 2 over 1 16 over 15 Pull
6-5 and 16-15	5 over 16 15 over 5 16 over 6 Pin 6 over 15 5 over 6 15 over 16 Pull
9-10 and 15-16	10 over 15 16 over 10 15 over 9 Pin 9 over 16 10 over 9 16 over 15 Pull
14-13 and 16-15	13 over 16 15 over 13 16 over 14 Pin 14 over 15 13 over 14 15 over 16 Pull
17-18 and 15-16	18 over 15 16 over 18 15 over 17 Pin 17 over 16 18 over 17 16 over 15 Pull
19-20 and 16-15	20 over 16 15 over 20 16 over 19 Pin 19 over 15 20 ove 19

	15 over 16 Pull
NEW ROW!!! 7-8 and 12-11	8 over 12 11 over 8 12 over 7 Pin 7 over 11 8 over 7 11 over 12 Pull
4-3 and 11-12	3 over 11 12 over 3 11 over 4 Pin 4 over 12 3 over 4 12 over 11 Pull
2-1 and 12-11	1 over 12 11 over 1 12 over 2 Pin 2 over 11 1 over 2 11 over 12 Pull
5-6 and 11-12	6 over 11 12 over 6 11 over 5 Pin 5 over 12 6 over 5 12 over 11 Pull
10-9 and 12-11	9 over 12 11 over 9 12 over 10 Pin 10 over 11 9 over 10 11 over 12 Pull
13-14 and 11-12	14 over 11 12 over 14 11 over 13 Pin 13 over 12 14 over 13

	12 over 11 Pull
18-17 and 12-11	17 over 12 11 over 17 12 over 18 Pin 18 over 11 17 over 18 11 over 12 Pull
20-19 and 11-12	19 over 11 12 over 19 11 over 20 Pin 20 over 12 19 over 20 12 over 11 Pull
15-16 and 12-11	16 over 12 11 over 16 12 over 15 Pin 15 over 11 16 over 15 11 over 12 Pull
NEW ROW!!! 3-4 and 8-7	4 over 8 7 over 4 8 over 3 Pin 3 over 7 4 over 3 7 over 8 Pull
1-2 and 7-8	2 over 7 8 over 2 7 over 1 Pin 1 over 8 2 over 1 8 over 7 Pull
6-5 and 8-7	5 over 8 7 over 5 8 over 6 Pin 6 over 7 5 over 6

	7 over 8 Pull
9-10 and 7-8	10 over 7 8 over 10 7 over 9 Pin 9 over 8 10 over 9 8 over 7 Pull
14-13 and 8-7	13 over 8 7 over 13 8 over 14 Pin 14 over 7 13 over 14 7 over 8 Pull
17-18 and 7-8	18 over 7 8 over 18 7 over 17 Pin 17 over 8 18 over 17 8 over 7 Pull
19-20 and 8-7	20 over 8 7 over 20 8 over 19 Pin 19 over 7 20 over 19 7 over 8 Pull
16-15 and 7-8	15 over 7 8 over 15 7 over 16 Pin 16 over 8 15 over 16 8 over 7 Pull

11-12 and 8-7	12 over 8 7 over 12 8 over 11 Pin 11 over 7 12 over 11 7 over 8 Pull

Pins should be in this order: 7-8; 12-11; 15-16; 19-20; 17-18; 13-14; 9-10; 5-6; 2-1; 4-3

At this point, you should have 5 full rows left to complete. The remaining 4 after that will not be using all the bobbins as we finish the bookmark off. Onto the last 5 full rows:

5th to Last Full Row: 2-1 and 4-3	1 over 4 3 over 1 4 over 2 Pin 2 over 3

	1 over 2 3 over 4 Pull
5-6 and 3-4	6 over 3 4 over 6 3 over 5 Pin 5 over 4 6 over 5 4 over 3 Pull
10-9 and 4-3	9 over 4 3 over 9 4 over 10 Pin 10 over 3 9 over 10 3 over 4 Pull
13-14 and 3-4	14 over 3 4 over 14 3 over 13 Pin 13 over 4 14 over 13 4 over 3 Pull
18-17 and 4-3	17 over 4 3 over 17 4 over 18 Pin 18 over 3 17 over 18 3 over 4 Pull
20-19 and 3-4	19 over 3 4 over 19 3 over 20 Pin 20 over 4 19 over 20 4 over 3 Pull
15-16 and 4-3	16 over 4 3 over 16 4 over 15 Pin

	15 over 3 16 over 15 3 over 4 Pull
12-11 and 3-4	11 over 3 4 over 11 3 over 12 Pin 12 over 4 11 over 12 4 over 3 Pull
7-8 and 4-3	8 over 4 3 over 8 4 over 7 Pin 7 over 3 8 over 7 3 over 4 Pull
4th to Last Full Row: 6-5 and 1-2	5 over 1 2 over 5 1 over 6 Pin 6 over 2 5 over 6 2 over 1 Pull
9-10 and 2-1	10 over 2 1 over 10 2 over 9 Pin 9 over 1 10 over 9 1 over 2 Pull
14-13 and 1-2	13 over 1 2 over 13 1 over 14 Pin 14 over 2 13 over 14 2 over 1 Pull
17-18 and 2-1	18 over 2 1 over 18 2 over 17 Pin

	17 over 1
	18 over 17
	1 over 2
	Pull
19-20 and 1-2	20 over 1
	2 over 20
	1 over 19
	Pin
	19 over 2
	20 over 19
	2 over 1
	Pull
16-15 and 2-1	15 over 2
	1 over 15
	2 over 16
	Pin
	16 over 1
	15 over 16
	1 over 2
	Pull
11-12 and 1-2	12 over 1
	2 over 12
	1 over 11
	Pin
	11 over 2
	12 over 11
	2 over 1
	Pull
8-7 and 2-1	7 over 2
	1 over 7
	2 over 8
	Pin
	8 over 1
	7 over 8
	1 over 2
	Pull
3-4 and 1-2	4 over 1
	2 over 4
	1 over 3
	Pin
	3 over 2
	4 over 3
	2 over 1
	Pull
3rd to Last Full Row: 10-9 and 5-6	9 over 5
	6 over 9
	5 over 10
	Pin

	10 over 6 9 over 10 6 over 5 Pull
13-14 and 6-5	14 over 6 5 over 14 6 over 13 Pin 13 over 5 14 over 13 5 over 6 Pull
18-17 and 5-6	17 over 5 6 over 17 5 over 18 Pin 18 over 6 17 over 18 6 over 5 Pull
20-19 and 6-5	19 over 6 5 over 19 6 over 20 Pin 20 over 5 19 over 20 5 over 6 Pull
15-16 and 5-6	16 over 5 6 over 16 5 over 15 Pin 15 over 6 16 over 15 6 over 5 Pull
12-11 and 6-5	11 over 6 5 over 11 6 over 12 Pin 12 over 5 11 over 12 5 over 6 Pull
7-8 and 5-6	8 over 5 6 over 8 5 over 7 Pin

	7 over 6
	8 over 7
	6 over 5
	Pull
4-3 and 6-5	3 over 6
	5 over 3
	6 over 4
	Pin
	4 over 5
	3 over 4
	5 over 6
	Pull
2-1 and 5-6	1 over 5
	6 over 1
	5 over 2
	Pin
	2 over 6
	1 over 2
	6 over 5
	Pull
2nd to Last Full Row: 14-13 and 9-10	13 over 9
	10 over 13
	9 over 14
	Pin
	14 over 10
	13 over 14
	10 over 9
	Pull
17-18 and 10-9	18 over 10
	9 over 18
	10 over 17
	Pin
	17 over 9
	18 over 17
	9 over 10
	Pull
19-20 and 9-10	20 over 9
	10 over 20
	9 over 19
	Pin
	19 over 10
	20 over 19
	10 over 9
	Pull
16-15 and 10-9	15 over 10
	9 over 15
	10 over 16
	Pin

	16 over 9
	15 over 16
	9 over 10
	Pull
11-12 and 9-10	12 over 9
	10 over 12
	9 over 11
	Pin
	11 over 10
	12 over 11
	10 over 9
	Pull
8-7 and 10-9	7 over 10
	9 over 7
	10 over 8
	Pin
	8 over 9
	7 over 8
	9 over 10
	Pull
3-4 and 9-10	4 over 9
	10 over 4
	9 over 3
	Pin
	3 over 10
	4 over 3
	10 over 9
	Pull
1-2 and 10-9	2 over 10
	9 over 2
	10 over 1
	Pin
	1 over 9
	2 over 1
	9 over 10
	Pull
6-5 and 9-10	5 over 9
	10 over 5
	9 over 6
	Pin
	6 over 10
	5 over 6
	10 over 9
	Pull
Last Full Row: 18-17 and 13-14	17 over 13
	14 over 17
	13 over 18
	Pin

	18 over 14
17 over 18
14 over 13
Pull
19-20 and 14-13	20 over 14
13 over 20
14 over 19
Pin
19 over 13
20 over 19
13 over 14
Pull
15-16 and 13-14	16 over 13
14 over 16
13 over 15
Pin
15 over 14
16 over 15
14 over 13
Pull
12-11 and 14-13	11 over 14
13 over 11
14 over 12
Pin
12 over 13
11 over 12
13 over 14
Pull
7-8 and 13-14	8 over 13
14 over 8
13 over 7
Pin
7 over 14
8 over 7
14 over 13
Pull
4-3 and 14-13	3 over 14
13 over 3
14 over 4
Pin
4 over 13
3 over 4
13 over 14
Pull
2-1 and 13-14	1 over 13
14 over 1
13 over 2
Pin

	2 over 14 1 over 2 14 over 13 Pull
5-6 and 14-13	6 over 14 13 over 6 14 over 5 Pin 5 over 13 6 over 5 13 over 14 Pull
10-9 and 13-14	9 over 13 14 over 9 13 over 10 Pin 10 over 14 9 over 10 14 over 13 Pull

Pins should be in this order: 14-13; 9-10; 6-5; 1-2; 3-4; 8-7; 11-12; 16-15; 20-19; 17-18	
Now we're at the partial rows to end the bookmark. You won't be using all the bobbin pairs anymore.	
1st Partial Row: 20-19 and 17-18	19 over 17 18 over 19 17 over 20

	Pin
	20 over 18
	19 over 20
	18 over 17
	Pull
16-15 and 18-17	15 over 18
	17 over 15
	18 over 16
	Pin
	16 over 17
	15 over 16
	17 over 18
	Pull
11-12 and 17-18	12 over 17
	18 over 12
	17 over 11
	Pin
	11 over 18
	12 over 11
	18 over 17
	Pull
8-7 and 18-17	7 over 18
	17 over 7
	18 over 8
	Pin
	8 over 17
	7 over 8
	17 over 18
	Pull
3-4 and 17-18	4 over 17
	18 over 4
	17 over 3
	Pin
	3 over 18
	4 over 3
	18 over 17
	Pull
1-2 and 18-17	2 over 18
	17 over 2
	18 over 1
	Pin
	1 over 17
	2 over 1
	17 over 18
	Pull
6-5 and 17-18	5 over 17
	18 over 5
	17 over 6

	Pin 6 over 18 5 over 6 18 over 17 Pull
9-10 and 18-17	10 over 18 17 over 10 18 over 9 Pin 9 over 17 10 over 9 17 over 18 Pull
14-13 and 17-18	13 over 17 18 over 13 17 over 14 Pin will be at the corner of the template. (See photo.) 14 over 18 13 over 14 18 over 17 Pull
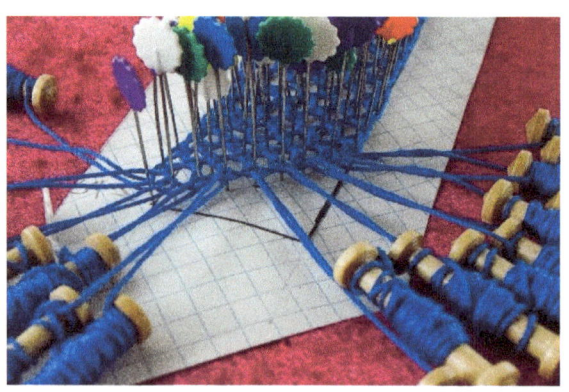	
2nd Partial Row: 15-16 and 19-20	16 over 19 20 over 16 19 over 15 Pin 15 over 20 16 over 15 20 over 19 Pull
12-11 and 20-19	11 over 20 19 over 11 20 over 12 Pin

	12 over 19 11 over 12 19 over 20 Pull
7-8 and 19-20	8 over 19 20 over 8 19 over 7 Pin 7 over 20 8 over 7 20 over 19 Pull
4-3 and 20-19	3 over 20 19 over 3 20 over 4 Pin 4 over 19 3 over 4 19 over 20 Pull
2-1 and 19-20	1 over 19 20 over 1 19 over 2 Pin 2 over 20 1 over 2 20 over 19 Pull
5-6 and 20-19	6 over 20 19 over 6 20 over 5 Pin will go at the bottom on the template. (See photo below.) 5 over 19 6 over 5 19 over 20 Pull
Last 2 pin sets: 10-9 and 19-20	9 over 19 20 over 9 19 over 10 Pin will go in the middle of the diamond. (See photo.)

	10 over 20 9 over 10 20 over 19 Pull

You won't be using pin sets: 18-17 and 13-14 after this.

3rd Partial Row: 11-12 and 16-15	12 over 16 15 over 12 16 over 11 Pin 11 over 15 12 over 11 15 over 16 Pull
8-7 and 15-16	7 over 15 16 over 7 15 over 8 Pin 8 over 16 7 over 8 16 over 15 Pull
3-4 and 16-15	4 over 16 15 over 4 16 over 3 Pin 3 over 15 4 over 3 15 over 16 Pull
1-2 and 15-16	2 over 15 16 over 2 15 over 1

	Pin 1 over 16 2 over 1 16 over 15 Pull
Last 2 pin sets: 6-5 and 16-15 You won't be using pin sets: 18-17; 13-14; 20-19; 9-10 after this.	5 over 16 15 over 5 16 over 6 Pin will go in the middle of the diamond along the template line. 6 over 15 5 over 6 15 over 16 Pull
4th Partial Row: 7-8 and 12-11	8 over 12 11 over 8 12 over 7 Pin 7 over 11 8 over 7 11 over 12 Pull
4-3 and 11-12	3 over 11 12 over 3 11 over 4 Pin 4 over 12 3 over 4 12 over 11 Pull
Last 2 pin sets: 2-1 and 12-11 You won't be using pin sets: 18-17; 13-14; 20-19; 9-10; 15-16; 5-6 after this.	1 over 12 11 over 1 12 over 2 Pin will go in middle of diamond along template line. 2 over 11 1 over 2 11 over 12 Pull
LAST ROW! Final 2 sets: 8-7 and 11-12 You're only using these 2 sets. Follow steps then proceed to finishing instructions.	7 over 11 12 over 7 11 over 8 Pin along the bottom of template. 8 over 12 7 over 8

| | 12 over 11 |
| | Pull |

You've made it to the end. Now we'll tie off the ends and you will have completed your first project.

To tie off, we're going to be working with 4 bobbins at a time, starting left to right. Undo the slipknots and unravel the thread on bobbins 18-17 & 13-14. Gather the threads and carefully tie a knot as close to the pins as possible.

Repeat for bobbins 20-19 & 9-10; 15-16 & 5-6; 11-12 & 1-2; and 7-8 & 4-3.

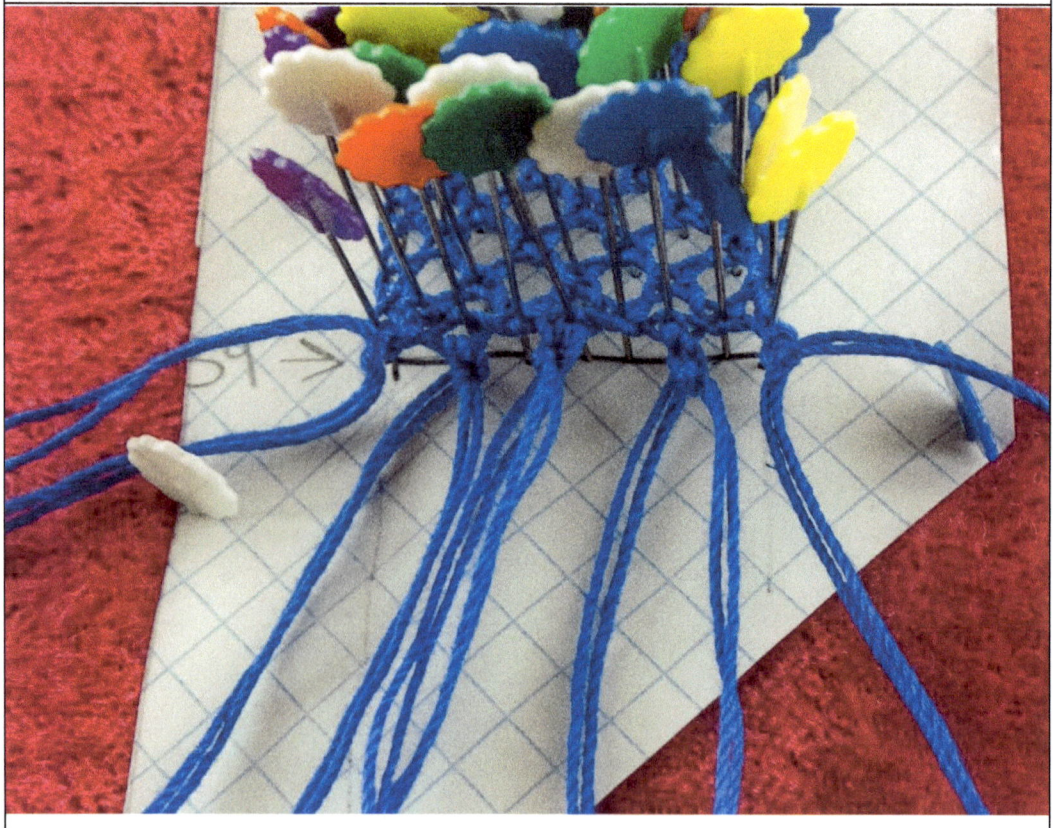

Carefully pull all the straight pins out of the piece.

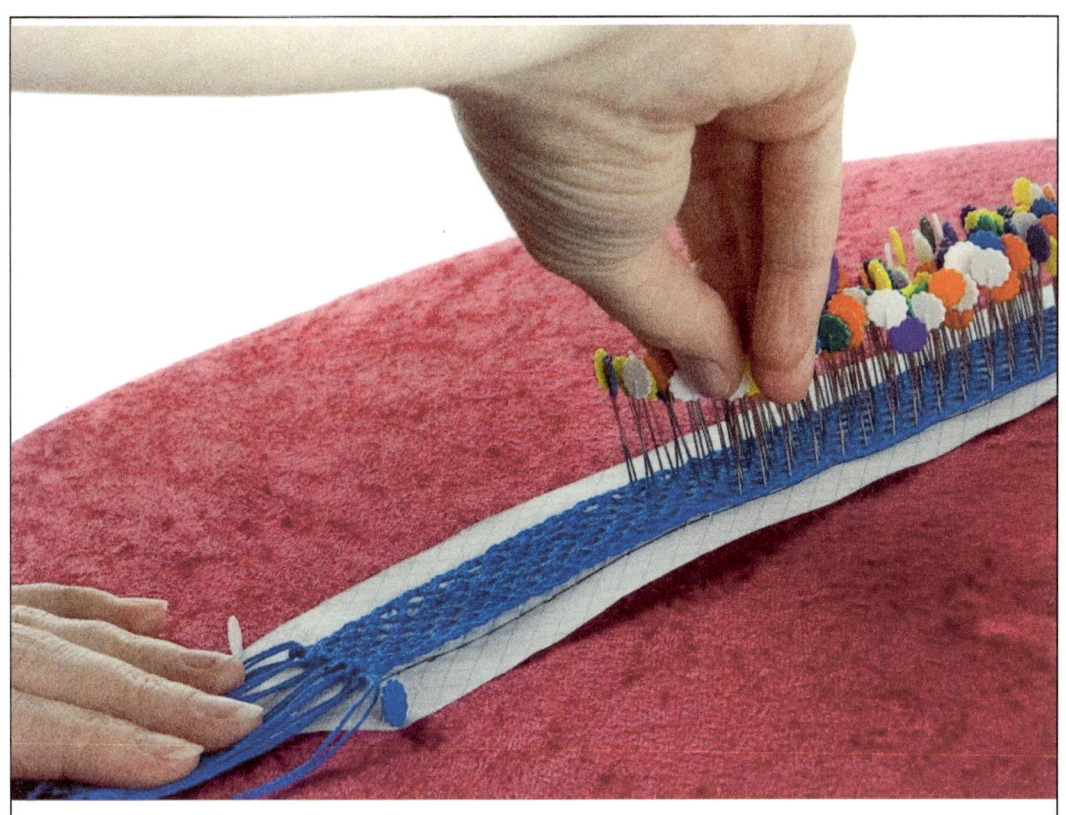

Unpin the piece at the top, and knot the strands, 4 together at a time.

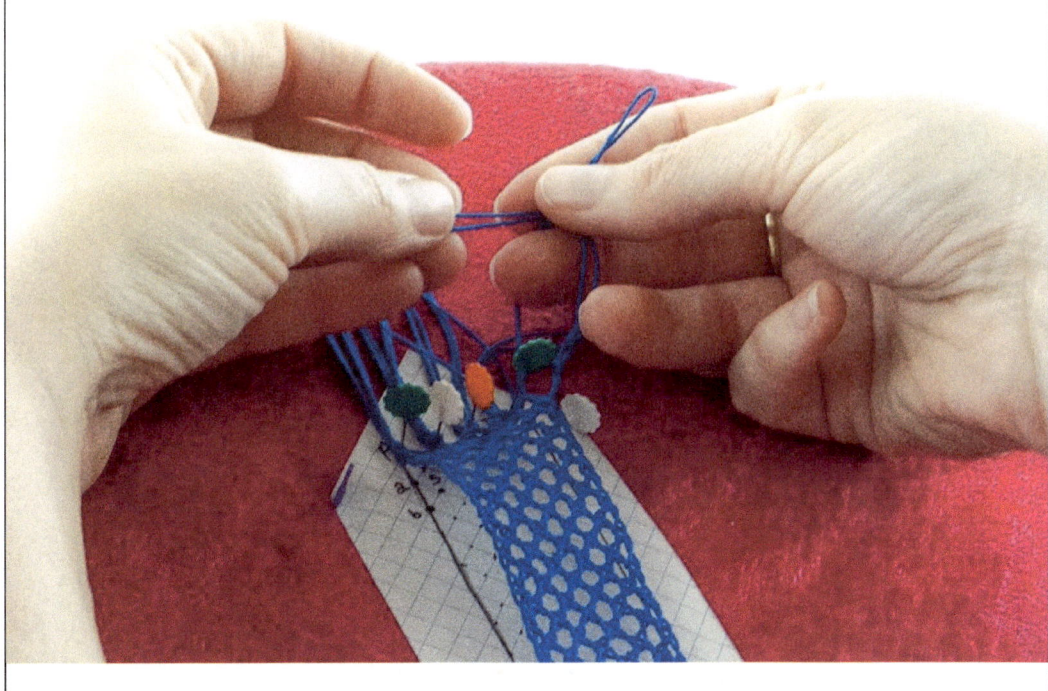

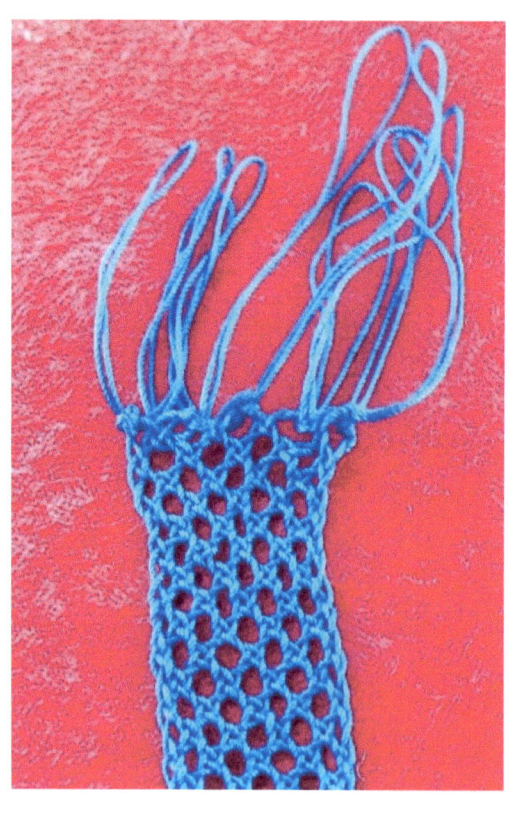

Using scissors, cut the loops open. Trim the excess thread off each end.

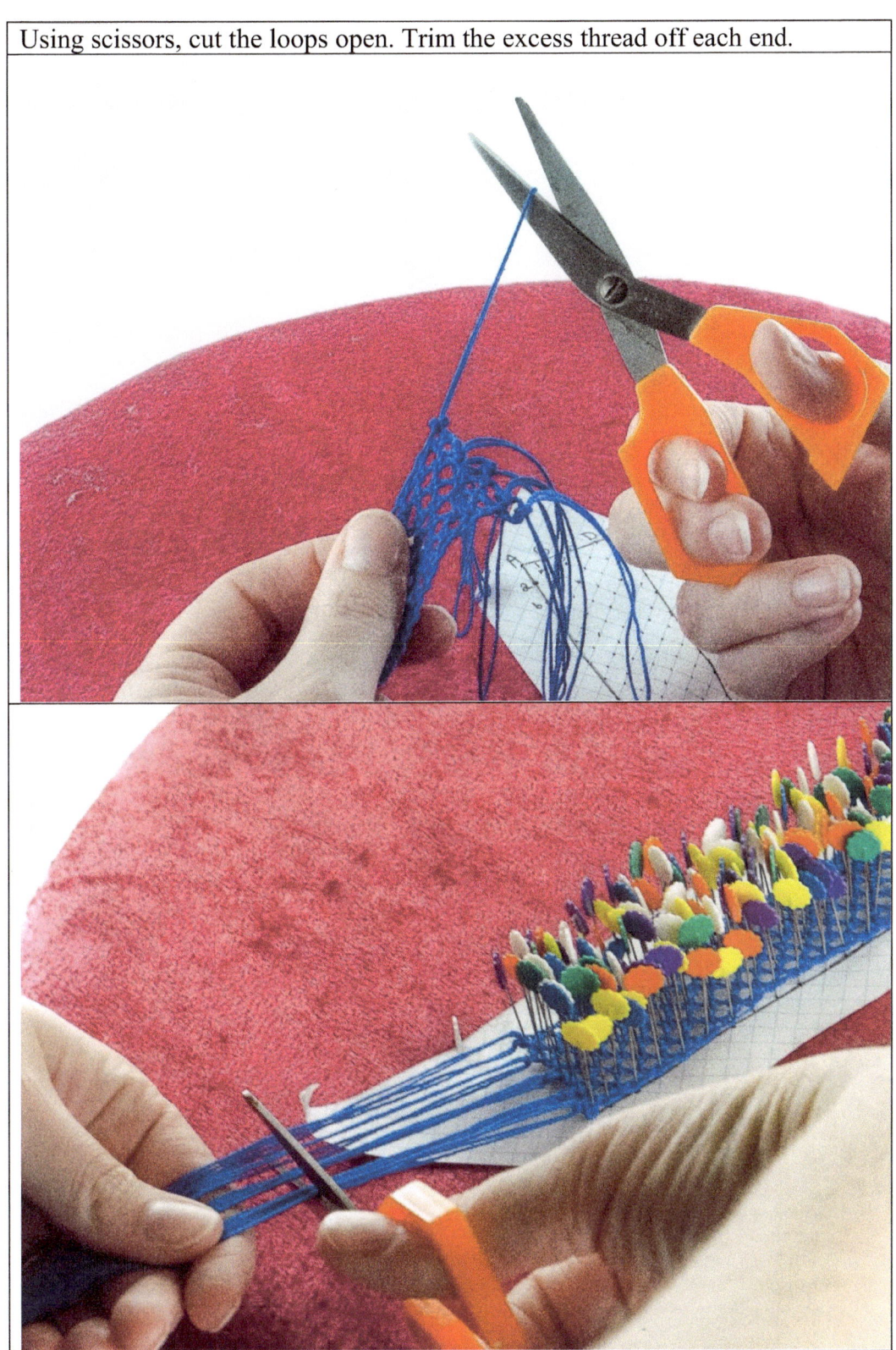

CONGRATULATIONS!!! You've just completed your first bookmark! Show it off! Use it! Make more for Christmas presents!

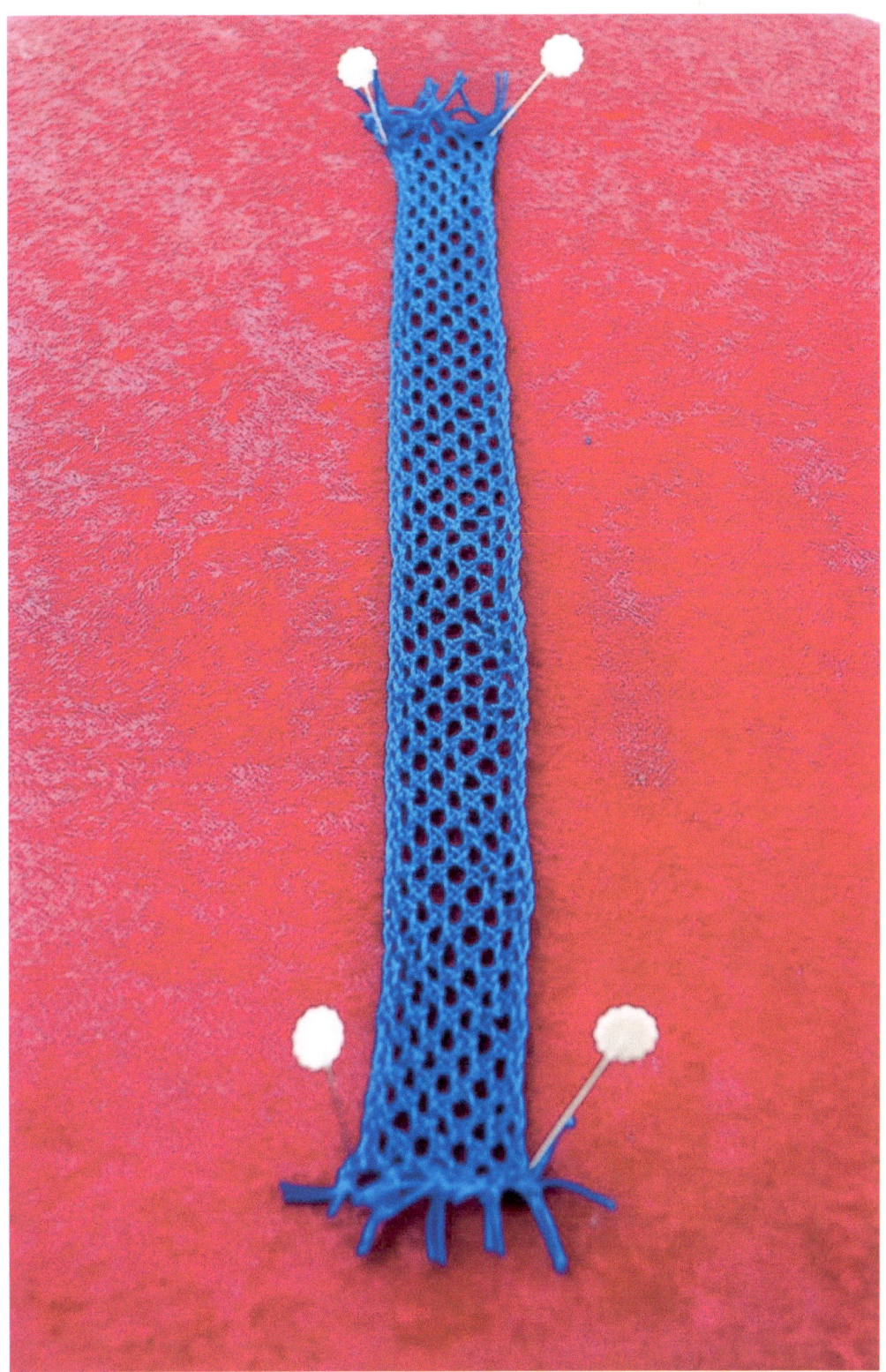

Notes Page:

Recommended Books & Other Resources

Books:

Beginner's Guide to Bobbin Lace by Gilian Dye
ISBN 9781844481088

Bobbin Lace: an Illustrated Guide to Traditional and Contemporary Techniques by Brigita Fuhrmann
ISBN 9780486249025

The Bobbin Lace Manual by Geraldine Scott
ISBN 9780486261942

How to Make Bobbin Lace by Jo Edkins
ASIN-B008ZC8YKS

Online Resources:

The Freeway Lace Guild
http://freewaylaceguild.org

International Organization of Lace, Inc.
http://www.internationalorganizationoflace.org

The Lace Guild Museum
www.laceguild.org

Lace Organizations, Guild Organizations, and Publications
www.bobbinmaker.com

Stourbridge Lace Guild
http://www.laceguild.org

Van Sciver Bobbin Lace
http://vansciverbobbinlace.com

YouTube Channels:

CraftHouseMagic
LouWoo
KnittingAllTheBlankets
TheLaceMakerDiary
RedCardinalCrafts

Notes Page:

Bibliography

Barry, Ann. "Shopper's World; Handmade Lace from Normandy." *New York Times*, October 13, 1985. *Gale Academic Onefile* (accessed December 18, 2019). https://link-gale-com.db22.linccweb.org/apps/doc/A176508750/AONE?u=lincclin_pcc&sid=AONE&xid=326229e1.

Byron, Ellen. "Delicate Task: In India, Women Work to Preserve the Craft of Lace; Even with Low-Cost Labor, Making It by Hand Is a Difficult Business; Keeping Dust, Chickens Away." *Wall Street Journal*, February 14, 2006. https://doi.org/http://db22.linccweb.org/login?url=https://search-proquest-com.db22.linccweb.org/docview/398952341?accountid=40333

Mullen, Maureen. "Lacemaking: Alive and Gaining Strength." *New York Times*, August 16, 1987. *Gale General OneFile* (accessed December 18, 2019). https://link-gale-com.db22.linccweb.org/apps/doc/A176094051/ITOF?u=lincclin_pcc&sid=ITOF&xid=1d62e366.

Parmal, Pamela A. "Lace." In *Encyclopedia of Clothing and Fashion*, edited by Valerie Steele, 323-327. Vol. 2. Detroit, MI: Charles Scribner's Sons, 2005. *Gale In Context: World History* (accessed December 18, 2019). https://link-gale-com.db22.linccweb.org/apps/doc/CX3427500351/WHIC?u=lincclin_pcc&sid=WHIC&xid=ad46205b.

The Reader's Digest Association, Inc. "Bobbin Lace." In *Reader's Digest Complete Guide to Needlework*, 426–34. Pleasantville, NY: The Reader's Digest Association, Inc., 1979.

Rogers, Kathleen. "The Labyrinths of Lace." *Women's Art Magazine*, no. 43 (November 1991): 16–17. http://search.ebscohost.com.db22.linccweb.org/login.aspx?direct=true&db=asu&AN=36277057&site=eds-live.

Notes Page:

About the Author

Cori Large is a writer, knitter, blogger, YouTuber, and librarian. She's been published several times in PaperPlanning e-magazine. When not working on her fictional worlds, nonfiction pieces, blog posts, filming YouTube videos, writing fiction, or knitting, she is taming research dragons as an academic librarian.

Website: http://caendicott.wordpress.com

TalesFromAPolkCountyGirl YouTube channel:
https://www.youtube.com/channel/UCwETw4Z0geZ52u9AErAZJwg

KnittingAllTheBlankets Knitting Podcast on YouTube:
https://www.youtube.com/channel/UCbwh5oIhRXL83y___mL2gSQ

InstaGram: @cori.large

Facebook page: https://www.facebook.com/talesfromapolkcountygirl/

Notes Page:

www.ingramcontent.com/pod-product-compliance
Lightning Source LLC
Chambersburg PA
CBHW042022150426
43198CB00002B/43